A Path of Love to Authentic Faith

INTRODUCTION TO WESTERN ORTHODOXY

D1715732

By Rev. Michael Callahan

AUTHENTIC FAITH SERIES #5

Imprimatur

By the grace of Almighty God as the Metropolitan Archbishop of the Archdiocese of New York for the Holy Orthodox Catholic and Apostolic Church of America, I am pleased to grant this Imprimatur to the book entitled *Introduction to Western Orthodoxy*, authored by His Grace, Bishop Michael Callahan.

This work is a valuable resource for those seeking to deepen their understanding of the Western Orthodox Christian tradition, grounded in Ancient Faith First Principles and free from the innovations and relativistic tendencies of our modern age. Bishop Callahan has written this text with great care, drawing upon the wisdom of the Apostles, the Church Fathers, and the undivided Church of the first millennium to present an authentic path for those yearning for a return to the fullness of the faith.

Introduction to Western Orthodoxy meets the high standards of orthodoxy and fidelity to the teachings of our Lord and Savior, Jesus Christ. This text has been thoroughly reviewed and found to be free of doctrinal error. As such, it is suitable for catechetical instruction and spiritual formation within the Holy Orthodox Catholic and Apostolic Church of America.

May all who read this book be blessed with deeper insight into the richness of the Orthodox Christian faith, and may it serve as a beacon of truth, guiding the faithful along the narrow way that leads to eternal life.

Given at New York, on this 1st day of November, being the Feast of All Saints, in the year of our Lord, 2024.

+ Anthony

Metropolitan Archbishop of New York

Holy Orthodox Catholic and Apostolic Church of America

Acknowledgments

I begin this work by giving thanks to Almighty God, whose boundless grace has guided me along this path, prompting me to embrace and defend Christian First Principles. It is through His mercy and wisdom that I have been led to the richness of the ancient faith and to the responsibility of sharing its profound truth with others. To Him be all glory, honor, and praise, now and forever.

I extend my deepest gratitude to His Excellency, Archbishop Anthony, whose trust and encouragement have been vital to my journey into Orthodoxy. His faith in my calling to serve within the Holy Orthodox Catholic and Apostolic Church of America has been an immeasurable blessing. His guidance and mentorship have strengthened my resolve to uphold the unchanging Apostolic Faith in a time when truth is often obscured by modern distortions and relativism. Thank you, Your Excellency, for standing as a steadfast example of devotion to the ancient path and for allowing me the honor of bringing others to the fullness of the faith.

Finally, I thank all those who have supported me in creating this work. This book, part of the Authentic Faith Series, represents not only my journey but also a collective endeavor to rediscover and preserve the Apostolic Tradition. It is my hope and prayer that this volume will inspire others to seek an authentic, sacramental relationship with God through the life-giving path of Western Orthodoxy.

To all who read this work, may God bless you richly in your faith journey, and may His grace continually lead you along the narrow way to life eternal.

In Christ's love,

+Bishop Michael Callahan

Table of Contents

Copyright Page

Title: Introduction to Western Orthodoxy: A Journey into Authentic Faith

Author: Title: Introduction to Western Orthodoxy: A Journey into Authentic Faith

Author: Bishop Michael Callahan

Illustrations: Bishop Michael Callahan

Publisher: [Bishop Michael Callahan

Published Date: 2024

ISBN: 9798343806557
First Edition

This book is a work of Religious nonfiction. While every effort has been made to ensure accuracy, the publisher and author assume no responsibility for errors or omissions. The interpretations and conclusions expressed in this book are those of the author.

Introduction

The Narrow Way to Authentic Faith

Do you believe Jesus when He said the way to life is narrow and only a few find it (Matthew 7:14)? If so, wouldn't it be essential to seek the most authentic path toward eternity with God? In a time where moral relativism and spiritual confusion influence even churches, there is a need to rediscover the original faith of the Apostles— unchanging and faithful through the centuries. Western Orthodoxy offers a path back to the fullness of the Apostolic Tradition, embracing the sacramental life, prayer, and a commitment to spiritual growth through theosis— union with God.

This book—the fifth volume in Bishop Michael Callahan's "Authentic Faith Series"—serves as a cornerstone for catechumens, inquirers, and lifelong Orthodox Christians seeking deeper faith formation. It has been designed to be used as part of a Western Orthodox catechism program, particularly for parishes within the Holy Orthodox Catholic and Apostolic Church of America (HOCACA). However, it is also suitable for other Western Orthodox jurisdictions. This program guides believers through the teachings of the early Church, equipping them to participate fully in the sacramental life and develop an authentic relationship with God.

Overview of the Catechism Course

This catechism course is structured as a 16- to 18-week journey, providing a comprehensive introduction to Western Orthodoxy. The flow of the course is built around key topics that develop logically, moving from an introduction to the faith to participation in the sacraments and the process of spiritual growth (theosis). The curriculum is designed to immerse catechumens and inquirers in the life of the Church while addressing theological questions often raised by those from Protestant or Roman Catholic backgrounds.

Each week builds upon the previous, guiding participants toward a fuller understanding of Orthodox worship, theology, and spiritual practice. Every session includes readings from scripture and patristic writings, reflections, time for questions, and practical guidance for living the faith.

The course can be completed in 16 weeks for a standard catechism program, or expanded to 18 weeks to allow more time for certain topics or for Q&A sessions as needed.

Course Structure and Weekly Topics

Below is the outline of the catechism program, with suggested topics for each week.

Using This Book in the Catechism Course

This book serves as a primary resource for the catechism course, offering theological reflections, practical guidance, and insights into the life of the Church. Each chapter corresponds to a weekly session, providing background material, scripture readings, and multiple-choice review questions.

At the end of each session, the participants are invited to reflect in prayer and consider how the teachings of the week can be applied to their daily lives. This format encourages active engagement with the faith and fosters a deeper understanding of what it means to live as an Orthodox Christian.

Weeks 1–2: Introduction to Western Orthodoxy

Week 1: The Narrow Way and the Path to Salvation

Overview of Western Orthodoxy

Introduction to the Apostolic Faith preserved by the Orthodox Church

How Western Orthodoxy differs from Eastern Orthodoxy and Roman Catholicism

Week 2: Authentic Faith and Theosis—Union with God

The Orthodox understanding of theosis as the goal of the Christian life

Spiritual warfare and the role of grace and human effort (synergy)

Weeks 3–5: The Role of the Sacraments in Salvation

Week 3: Synergy—Cooperation Between Divine Grace and Human Effort

Exploring the relationship between grace and human effort

The role of asceticism and prayer in spiritual growth

Week 4: Baptism and Chrismation—Sacraments of Initiation

The importance of infant baptism and Chrismation

Comparison with Roman Catholic confirmation and Protestant views on baptism

Week 5: The Eucharist—The Source and Summit of Christian Life

The Orthodox understanding of the real presence of Christ in the Eucharist

John 6:53 and the necessity of the Eucharist for salvation

Weeks 6–8: Confession, Repentance, and Healing

Week 6: Confession and Repentance—The Sacrament of Healing

How confession heals the soul and aids spiritual growth

Comparison with Protestant views on sin and repentance

Week 7: Holy Matrimony—A Sacrament of Union and Path to Salvation

Marriage as an icon of Christ and the Church

The spiritual role of marriage in personal sanctification

Week 8: Holy Unction—Healing for Body and Soul

The sacrament of Holy Unction and its role in healing

Scriptural examples of healing and the ministry of the Church

Weeks 9–12: Living the Faith through Worship and Community

Week 9: The Church as the Mystical Body of Christ

The Church as the community of salvation

Comparison with Protestant views of the Church

Week 10: Holy Orders—The Sacrament of Apostolic Ministry

The role of bishops, priests, and deacons in the life of the Church

The concept of "in persona Christi" and the priest as a living icon of Christ

Week 11: The Liturgical Life—Gregorian and Sarum Rites

An introduction to the liturgical heritage of Western Orthodoxy

The difference between Gregorian and Sarum liturgies

Week 12: The Role of Icons in Orthodox Worship

Icons as windows to heaven and aids to prayer

The theological significance of icons

Weeks 13–15: Doctrine, Theology, and the Christian Life

Week 13: The Role of the Theotokos and the Saints

Veneration of the Virgin Mary and the saints

Comparison with Protestant objections and misunderstandings

Week 14: The Orthodox Understanding of Sin and Salvation

The difference between ancestral sin and original sin

How salvation is a process, not a one-time event

Week 15: Asceticism, Fasting, and Spiritual Warfare

How fasting and ascetic practices help believers grow in theosis

The role of spiritual warfare in the Christian life

Weeks 16–18: Final Reflections and Preparing for Reception into the Church

Week 16: Summary and Review of Orthodox Doctrine and Practices

A review of key teachings covered throughout the course

Addressing any remaining questions or concerns

Week 17 (Optional): The Sacraments and Their Ongoing Role in Salvation

How the sacraments continually shape the Christian life

The importance of regular participation in the Eucharist and Confession

Week 18 (Optional): Final Q&A and Preparing for Reception into the Church

Preparing catechumens for baptism or Chrismation

Celebrating the journey into full communion with the Church

An Invitation to Walk the Narrow Way

The journey of faith in Western Orthodoxy is one of love, transformation, and perseverance. It is not an easy path, but it is the one that Christ invites all believers to walk—a narrow way that leads to life (Matthew 7:14). Through prayer, participation in the sacraments, and the pursuit of theosis, believers are drawn closer to God and become partakers in the divine life.

This book, and the catechism course it accompanies, is an invitation to experience the fullness of the Orthodox faith—a faith that is unchanging, uncompromising, and overflowing with the grace of God. May it lead all who walk this path toward the joy of eternal communion with Him.

Introducton Concluding Prayer

O Lord Jesus Christ, guide us along the narrow way that leads to life. Strengthen us to walk faithfully in Your truth, seeking communion with You through prayer, repentance, and participation in the sacraments. May Your grace sustain us on this journey, and may we always grow in love for You and our neighbors. Through the prayers of the saints, now and ever, and unto ages of ages. Amen.

About the Author: Bishop Michael Callahan

I am Bishop Michael Callahan, Diocesan Bishop of Phoenix, Arizona, for the Holy Orthodox Catholic and Apostolic Church of America. Throughout my life and ministry, I have been committed to preserving and promoting the **Authentic Christian Faith** as it was practiced by the early Church. This focus has shaped my writings, teachings, and pastoral work, guiding others toward the ancient faith of the Orthodox Church.

This study guide is the fifth book in my ongoing **"Authentic Faith" series**, a collection that explores Christian theology, the sacraments, and the spiritual life from an Orthodox perspective. Each volume builds on the core principles of Orthodox Christianity, offering theological depth and practical insights for those seeking a faith rooted in tradition and empowered by grace.

My spiritual journey has taken me through various Christian traditions, yet I have always been drawn back to the enduring truth found in the ancient faith of Orthodoxy. As a bishop, my mission is to share this treasure with others and help them discover the richness of **Western**

Orthodoxy—a faith both ancient and alive, relevant today, and capable of transforming hearts and lives.

I pray that this book serves as a guide and inspiration for all seeking a deeper relationship with Christ. May it lead you closer to God, enrich your understanding of His love and grace, and help you experience the beauty and truth of the Orthodox Christian faith.

Dedication

To my **patient and loving wife** of many years, whose support and encouragement have been a constant source of strength on this journey.

To my **children and grandchildren**, with the prayer that you will grow to experience the fullness of **God's grace** through His sacramental love, finding joy and peace in walking the **narrow way** that leads to life.

May this book serve as a guide to discovering the beauty and depth of the **Apostolic Faith** and draw you ever closer to the One who loves us beyond measure.

Chapter 1:

Introduction to Western Orthodoxy
A Path of Love to Authentic Faith

Western Orthodoxy provides a path to rediscover the fullness of the ancient Christian faith within the context of Western cultural traditions. **The Holy Orthodox Catholic and Apostolic Church of America (HOCACA)** offers this expression of the faith, preserving the core teachings of the Apostolic Church while engaging meaningfully with modern Western society. In a time marked by **moral relativism** and shifting values, Western Orthodoxy offers stability, truth, and **authentic love for God and neighbor**.

This chapter introduces the theological and ecclesiological distinctiveness of Western Orthodoxy, particularly in relation to **Eastern Orthodoxy, Roman Catholicism,** and Protestantism. We will explore significant **theological developments** that occurred in the West, such as the addition of the **Filioque clause** to the Nicene Creed, the doctrine of **papal infallibility**, and the practice of **indulgences**. These developments, which Orthodoxy sees as innovations, are examined through the lens of the **Apostolic Tradition**, which the Orthodox Church has sought to preserve faithfully without alteration since the time of the early Church.

We begin with the story of **St. Herman of Alaska**, a beloved Orthodox saint whose life exemplifies **faithful love, service, and union with God**.

The Story of St. Herman of Alaska—A Life of Love and Authentic Faith

St. Herman of Alaska (c. 1750–1837) was born in Russia and began his spiritual journey as a monk in the **Valaam Monastery**. Over time, he felt called to participate in a mission to **Alaska**, where he would serve among the native peoples. When St. Herman and his fellow missionaries arrived in the unforgiving wilderness, they encountered not only the physical challenges of life in a new land but also the **mistreatment of the native people** by Russian traders.

St. Herman became a **fierce advocate for the oppressed**, defending the native Alaskans against injustice. He learned their language, lived among them, and treated them with the same dignity and love that Christ shows to all people. His life of prayer, asceticism, and service was rooted in a deep sense of **communion with God**. On **Spruce Island**, where he made his hermitage, St. Herman's life became a beacon of light to all who sought his guidance. His example teaches us that authentic Christian faith is more than belief—it is a life of **love, humility, and service to others**.

This is the spirit that Western Orthodoxy seeks to offer: a faith that is not defined by innovations or theological trends but one that remains rooted in the love of God, expressed through the **sacramental life** and the **pursuit of theosis**—union with God.

The Filioque Clause: A Prohibited Addition to the Creed

The **Filioque clause** was one of the earliest theological innovations that contributed to the growing divide between the **Eastern and Western Churches**. Originally, the **Nicene Creed** declared that the **Holy Spirit proceeds from the Father** (in accordance with John 15:26). However, in the **Latin-speaking West**, the phrase **"and the Son" (Filioque)** was added, resulting in a new formulation: "the Holy Spirit, who proceeds from the Father **and the Son**."

Why the Orthodox Church Rejects the Filioque

The Orthodox Church objects to the Filioque for both **theological** and **canonical** reasons:

1. **Distortion of Trinitarian Theology**

   In Orthodox theology, the **Father** is the sole source (or "principle") of both the **Son** and the **Holy Spirit**. The addition of the Filioque introduces a **dual**

procession, altering the Trinitarian relationship and confusing the roles of the persons of the Trinity. This change shifts the focus away from the Father as the unique source of both the Son and the Spirit.

2. **Violation of Conciliar Authority**

The **Third Ecumenical Council (Ephesus, 431)** prohibited any changes to the Creed. The Council declared:

"It is unlawful for any man to bring forward, or to write, or to compose a different (ἑτέραν) faith as a rival to that established by the holy Fathers assembled with the Holy Ghost in Nicaea."

The introduction of the Filioque in the West violated this canon by altering the Creed without the approval of an **ecumenical council**, undermining the Church's **conciliar structure**. The unilateral change became a source of tension between East and West, contributing to the **Great Schism of 1054**.

Papal Infallibility: An Orthodox Critique

The doctrine of **papal infallibility**, formally defined at the **First Vatican Council** in 1870, teaches that the Pope, when speaking **ex cathedra** on matters of faith and morals, is preserved from error by the Holy Spirit. This teaching reflects the Roman Catholic understanding of the Pope's supreme authority over the entire Church.

Orthodoxy rejects the concept of papal infallibility for several reasons:

1. **Authority Belongs to the Whole Church**

   In the Orthodox Church, authority is **collegial**, exercised through **councils of bishops** who collectively preserve the Apostolic Tradition. The Orthodox Church holds that the **Holy Spirit guides the entire Church**, not just one individual. Truth is discerned through the consensus of the Church, as seen in the ecumenical councils.

2. **The Infallibility of the Church, Not the Individual**

   Orthodoxy teaches that **the Church as a whole** is protected from error by the Holy Spirit. This protection extends to the faithful, the bishops, and the clergy working together as the Body of Christ. The elevation of the Pope to a position of infallibility, from the Orthodox perspective, introduces a **foreign concept** that departs from the Apostolic model of governance.

3. **A Cause of Division**

   The assertion of papal supremacy has been a major

factor in the division between the **Roman Catholic** and **Orthodox Churches**. Orthodox Christianity honors the Bishop of Rome as **first among equals** but does not recognize his jurisdiction over the entire Church.

The Orthodox Understanding of Indulgences

The Roman Catholic practice of **indulgences** emerged from the belief that the Church could grant **remission of temporal punishment** for sins, either for the living or the dead, based on the merits of Christ and the saints. This practice led to serious abuses, such as the **selling of indulgences**, which became a catalyst for the **Protestant Reformation**.

Why Orthodoxy Rejects Indulgences

Orthodoxy does not recognize the concept of indulgences for several reasons:

1. **Sin and Repentance as a Healing Process**

   In Orthodox theology, sin is understood as a **spiritual illness** that requires healing through **repentance** and participation in the **sacraments**, particularly **Confession** and the **Eucharist**. The focus is on **restoring communion with God**, not on satisfying a legal debt through indulgences.

2. **The Role of God's Mercy and Prayer**

   Orthodox Christians believe that **God's mercy** is freely given to those who repent. Prayers for the dead are offered as expressions of love and hope for their salvation, but the idea of **quantifying forgiveness** through indulgences is foreign to Orthodox theology.

3. **The Danger of Treating Forgiveness as a Transaction**

   The Orthodox Church emphasizes that **salvation is a process of transformation** (theosis), not a legal transaction. The concept of indulgences risks reducing forgiveness to a **mechanical act** rather than a personal encounter with God's grace.

Current Developments: The Synod on Synodality

As of this writing, the **Roman Catholic Church** is currently engaged in a process called the **Synod on Synodality**, which emphasizes listening to the laity and re-evaluating certain teachings and practices. While some see this as an opportunity for renewal, Orthodox Christians observe these developments with caution.

Orthodoxy holds that the **truth of the faith is unchanging** and cannot be altered to accommodate cultural trends or modern sensibilities. The teachings of the Church are **eternal**, reflecting the truth revealed by Christ and transmitted by the Apostles. Any attempt to **reinterpret doctrine** risks departing from the Apostolic Tradition.

Western Orthodoxy preserves and restores two primary liturgical forms, offering believers an opportunity to worship through rites that reflect both ancient Western traditions and the depth of the Apostolic Faith. These liturgies serve as a vital expression of Orthodox worship, immersing participants in prayer, sacred music, and sacramental grace. In the Holy Orthodox Catholic and Apostolic Church of America (HOCACA), the Gregorian Rite—in a faithful English translation of its original form—serves as the primary means of liturgical celebration. Both the Gregorian and Sarum Rites retain their distinctive characteristics, allowing worshipers to encounter the beauty of God through different, yet authentic, expressions of the faith.

Gregorian Rite: Ancient Simplicity Restored

The Gregorian Rite is rooted in the early liturgical practices of the Roman Church and is known for its solemnity and simplicity. In the Western Orthodox tradition, the Gregorian Rite emphasizes contemplative prayer through structured liturgy, with Gregorian chant playing a central role in fostering an atmosphere of reverence and stillness.

While this rite serves as the foundation for the Latin Mass in Roman Catholicism, the version used within Western Orthodoxy represents a restoration to its earlier, pre-Schism form, free from the later innovations introduced by the Roman Catholic Church. In this context, the Holy Orthodox Catholic and Apostolic Church of America uses a faithful English translation of the Gregorian Rite to make the liturgical heritage accessible to modern worshipers without compromising its ancient integrity.

The restored Gregorian Rite reflects the same spirit of Apostolic worship practiced in the early centuries—focused on simplicity, reverence, and immersion in the mystery of God's grace through the Eucharist.

Sarum Rite: A Liturgy Rich in Symbolism and Beauty

The Sarum Rite, developed in medieval England, offers a more ornate and ceremonial expression of the Western liturgical tradition. It reflects the liturgical heritage of the British Isles, with a focus on processions, hymns, and symbolic gestures that engage the senses and draw participants into the drama of salvation. This rite emphasizes the communal nature of worship, inviting the faithful to participate actively in the liturgical cycle of the Church.

While more elaborate than the Gregorian Rite, the Sarum Rite retains the same Orthodox theology and sacramental focus, emphasizing the real presence of Christ in the Eucharist. This rite is especially beloved by those drawn to visual beauty and ritual in worship, as it provides a richly textured experience of sacramental life.

Encountering Christ Through Both Rites

Both the Gregorian and Sarum Rites preserve the theological essence of the Orthodox faith, emphasizing the real presence of Christ in the Eucharist and inviting believers to participate in the mystery of God's grace. These rites are not merely aesthetic or cultural artifacts;

they are the means by which worshipers encounter the living God through the sacraments and are drawn into communion with Him.

By participating in either of these liturgies, believers are invited to enter the timeless worship of the Church, joining with the saints and angels in glorifying God. The Gregorian Rite, with its simplicity and chant, fosters quiet reflection and prayer, while the Sarum Rite, with its processions and symbolism, offers a vivid and engaging encounter with the divine. Together, these rites represent the rich diversity of Western Orthodoxy while remaining fully aligned with the Apostolic Tradition.

Western Orthodoxy thus offers a way for believers to experience the fullness of the Christian faith, expressed through ancient, restored forms of worship that emphasize the transformative power of the Eucharist and the beauty of God's sacramental grace.

Why Western Orthodoxy?

Western Orthodoxy offers a way to reconnect with the **Apostolic Faith**, free from the innovations introduced by the Roman Catholic Church and the theological fragmentation seen in Protestantism. It provides a path to

authentic faith through **prayer, asceticism, and the sacraments**, leading believers into **union with God**.

Chapter 1. Concluding Prayer

O Lord Jesus Christ, guide us on the path of love and truth. Help us remain faithful to the teachings entrusted to Your Church, that we may grow in Your grace and become partakers of Your divine nature. Through the prayers of St. Herman of Alaska and all the saints, may we walk faithfully in Your way, now and ever, and unto ages of ages. Amen.

Chapter 1 Review Questions

Why does the Orthodox Church reject the Filioque clause?

- o A) It was introduced without conciliar approval
- o B) It distorts the theology of the Trinity
- o C) It violates the canons of the Council of Ephesus
- o D) All of the above

What is the Orthodox view of indulgences?

- o A) They are necessary for salvation
- o B) They are a legitimate form of repentance
- o C) They are a transactional distortion of forgiveness
- o D) They are optional for devout Christians

This chapter sets the foundation for understanding how Western Orthodoxy offers a path to **authentic faith**, rooted in the teachings of the early Church and free from later theological innovations.

Chapter 2:

Introduction: Theosis and the Call to Transformation

In **Orthodox Christianity**, the ultimate goal of the Christian life is **theosis**—the process of **becoming one with God** by participating in His **divine nature** through grace. Theosis is not about becoming God by essence but about **growing in communion with Him** and being transformed into **His likeness**. This transformation occurs through **sacramental participation, prayer, fasting, repentance, and acts of love**.

For some from **Roman Catholic** or **Protestant backgrounds**, the concept of theosis may seem unfamiliar or challenging. Orthodox theology emphasizes that **theosis is not an attempt to attain divinity**, but rather a return to the unity with God for which humanity was originally created. As **2 Peter 1:4** teaches, believers are invited to become **"partakers of the divine nature."**

Orthodoxy encourages **daily repentance** and spiritual growth throughout life, focusing on the **transforming power of God's grace in the present**, rather than relying on a process of post-death purification. This teaching contrasts with the Roman Catholic concept of **purgatory**, which was introduced later in Church history.

The theology of **purgatory** in **Roman Catholicism** developed gradually between the **4th and 12th centuries** but only emerged as a fully defined doctrine **centuries**

after the Great Schism of 1054, which divided the Eastern and Western Churches. Early Christian thinkers, such as **St. Augustine**, hinted at the idea of **intermediate purification** after death. Influenced by his understanding of **original sin**—as both inherited guilt and personal fault—Augustine suggested that **even those forgiven in life** might still need purification after death.

However, purgatory did not become a formal doctrine until the **12th century**, when theologians like **St. Thomas Aquinas** provided a more systematic explanation, describing it as a process of **temporal punishment for sins**. The doctrine was officially recognized by the **Second Council of Lyon (1274)**, affirming that **souls of the faithful** could undergo post-death purification to prepare them for heaven. Later councils, such as the **Council of Florence (1439)** and the **Council of Trent (1545–1563)**, further refined and reinforced the belief that even those who die in God's grace may still need **purification from venial sins or the lingering effects of forgiven sins**—what Roman Catholicism terms **temporal punishment** (Catechism of the Catholic Church 1030–1032).

Roman Catholic doctrine emphasizes that **purgatory is not a second chance for salvation** but rather a **necessary cleansing process** before a soul can enter heaven. This belief flows from the idea that while **baptism removes the guilt of original sin**, it does not erase all the **temporal consequences of sin**. Thus, **purgatory** became a way to address this imbalance. Yet, this development **took shape centuries after the Great Schism**, cementing a growing theological divergence between the Roman Catholic Church and the **Orthodox East**.

Orthodoxy's View: Ancestral Sin and Rejection of Purgatory

In contrast, the **Orthodox Church** rejects the formal concept of purgatory, maintaining a theology rooted in the **sacramental life, repentance, and theosis**. Orthodoxy's rejection of purgatory reflects a different understanding of sin. Rather than teaching **original sin** as inherited guilt, Orthodoxy speaks of **ancestral sin**—the broken state of human nature inherited from Adam and Eve. In this view, sin is not passed down as guilt but as a **corruption that separates humanity from God**. Therefore, **Orthodoxy sees no need for an intermediary purification process** like purgatory. Instead, the focus is on **spiritual healing and transformation** during life, through **prayer, repentance, fasting, and the sacraments**.

Orthodoxy emphasizes that **God's grace and mercy are sufficient to purify and transform believers within the Church**, allowing them to grow in holiness through participation in **the life of the Church**. The goal is **theosis**—the lifelong process of becoming more like God through **synergistic cooperation between divine grace and human effort**. For Orthodox Christians, this **healing process must occur now**—in this life—not through a postmortem state of punishment but through the transformative power of the sacraments.

Prayers for the Departed: The Orthodox Approach to the Afterlife

While the Orthodox Church does not teach a doctrine of purgatory, it recognizes the importance of **praying for the departed**. These prayers are understood as acts of love and intercession, asking God to show mercy on the souls of those who have passed. However, **Orthodoxy does not teach a fixed place or state of purification after death**. Instead, the emphasis remains on **the present life** as the time for repentance, healing, and preparation for union with God.

Orthodox prayers for the dead reflect a belief that **God's mercy transcends time**, and **the Church, both on**

earth and in heaven, remains connected through these prayers. However, the focus is not on satisfying temporal punishments but on asking **God to draw the departed closer to His light and love**.

Diverging Theologies: Post-Schism Developments and Differences

The development of **purgatory** in Roman Catholicism exemplifies how the **West and East diverged** theologically after the **Great Schism of 1054**. Roman Catholicism's focus on **original sin** and the need for **temporal punishment** shaped the doctrine of purgatory as a necessary postmortem process. In contrast, Orthodoxy's emphasis on **ancestral sin** and the sacramental life leaves no room for a concept like purgatory. Instead, **theosis**—the gradual transformation into the likeness of God—remains central to the Orthodox understanding of salvation.

While both traditions encourage **prayers for the dead**, they do so with different theological foundations. Roman Catholicism views **purgatory as a continuation of sanctification**, addressing the consequences of sin, while Orthodoxy focuses on **spiritual growth and healing** in this life. For Orthodoxy, the time for **preparation and repentance** is now, not after death.

Conclusion: Orthodox Christianity's Timeless Emphasis on Theosis

The doctrine of purgatory reflects a **Western development** that emerged after the Great Schism, diverging from the **early Apostolic tradition** preserved in the Orthodox Church. While the Roman Catholic Church sought to **systematize salvation** through doctrines like purgatory, Orthodoxy has remained faithful to the belief that **salvation is a transformative journey**—one that takes place within the **sacramental life of the Church**.

Ultimately, **Orthodoxy rejects the notion of a postmortem purification process** because **God's grace, accessed through the sacraments, is sufficient for healing and transformation** during this life. **Theosis**, the process of becoming one with God, is the Orthodox goal of the Christian life—a goal that begins now and extends into eternity.

The Story of St. Patrick: A Journey of Theosis

The life of **St. Patrick of Ireland** illustrates the path of **theosis** through **prayer, repentance, and obedience** to God's will. Born in **Roman Britain**, Patrick was kidnapped by Irish pirates at the age of 16 and sold into slavery. During his captivity, Patrick experienced a profound **spiritual awakening**. Isolated and suffering, he turned to **prayer**, spending long hours contemplating God's mercy. Patrick later wrote:

"The love of God and His fear increased in me more and more, and my faith grew."

After six years in captivity, Patrick escaped and returned to his family, but he did not return to an ordinary life. Instead, he committed himself to **God's service**, eventually becoming a monk. Years later, Patrick had a vision in which the **Irish people called him to return** and bring the Gospel to them. Despite the dangers, Patrick obeyed, returning to the land of his former captors to share **Christ's love**. His life exemplifies **synergism**—the cooperation between **divine grace and human effort**—and the process of **theosis**, not just in personal transformation but in bringing transformation to others.

Theosis: Participating in the Divine Nature

Theosis is not merely about moral improvement or following religious rules. It is about **being healed and** transformed by God's grace so that we reflect His image and likeness. Through His **uncreated energies**, God shares His divine life with us, enabling us to grow in **holiness and communion** with Him. This process begins at **baptism**, where believers are united with **Christ's death and resurrection**, and continues through **prayer, repentance, participation in the Eucharist, and ascetic practices**.

Unlike the **Roman Catholic view of sanctification** as a process that may continue after death in purgatory, Orthodoxy teaches that **spiritual renewal must happen in this life**. Theosis invites believers to actively cooperate with God's grace every day, experiencing purification through the sacraments and spiritual disciplines.

Synergism: Cooperation Between Divine Grace and Human Effort

In Orthodox theology, **synergism** refers to the **dynamic cooperation between God's grace and human effort** in the process of salvation. While salvation is initiated by God, believers are called to respond through **faith, prayer, repentance, and love**. As St. Paul teaches in **Philippians 2:12-13**,

"Work out your own salvation with fear and trembling, for it is God who works in you, both to will and to work for His good pleasure."

St. Patrick's life demonstrates the importance of **synergism**. While God's grace called him to conversion, it was **Patrick's faithful response** through prayer, fasting, and missionary work that allowed this grace to bear fruit. His transformation shows that **theosis is a journey requiring both divine grace and human cooperation**.

Asceticism: Spiritual Discipline on the Path to Theosis

Asceticism—the practice of spiritual discipline—plays a vital role in theosis. Through fasting, prayer, almsgiving, and self-denial, believers discipline their bodies and souls, making them more receptive to **God's transforming grace**. In Orthodoxy, asceticism is not about earning God's favor but about **purifying the heart** and redirecting our desires toward Him.

Patrick's time in captivity served as a form of **ascetic training**, preparing him for the mission that God would later entrust to him. Through suffering, prayer, and fasting,

Patrick experienced **inner purification** and grew closer to God, embodying the Orthodox understanding of **theosis through ascetic practice**.

Prayer, Sacraments, and Icons in the Journey of Theosis

Prayer and the sacraments are essential tools on the path of theosis. In prayer, we enter into **communion with God**, allowing His grace to transform us. In the **Eucharist**, we receive the very Body and Blood of Christ, nourishing our souls for the journey toward theosis. **Confession** offers healing and renewal, allowing believers to remove obstacles that hinder their growth in holiness.

Icons also play an essential role, serving as windows to heaven. They remind believers of their call to become **living icons of Christ** and inspire them to grow in **holiness and communion with God**.

Conclusion: Theosis vs. Purgatory—A Life of Transformation in the Present

In **Orthodox Christianity**, theosis is the heart of the Christian life. It is the process by which believers are transformed by grace, becoming **partakers of the divine nature**. Unlike the Roman Catholic concept of **purgatory**, which teaches that purification may occur after death, Orthodoxy emphasizes **spiritual renewal during this life** through **prayer, repentance, and participation in the sacraments**.

The journey of **theosis** invites every believer to cooperate with God's grace through **synergism**, embracing the spiritual disciplines that lead to transformation. The story of **St. Patrick** shows that even in suffering, prayer, and obedience, we can experience the fullness of God's grace and bring transformation to the world.

Chapter 2. Concluding Prayer

O Lord, who calls us to share in Your divine nature, guide us on the path of theosis. Help us to open our hearts to Your grace and cooperate with Your will. Through the prayers of St. Patrick and all the saints, may we grow in love, humility, and holiness, becoming more like You. Amen.

Chapter 2. Chapter Review Questions

What is theosis in Orthodox theology?

- o **A) The process of becoming like God and sharing in His divine nature**
- o B) A state of moral perfection
- o C) A theological abstraction
- o D) A concept for monks only

When did the theology of purgatory become a formal doctrine in the Roman Church?

- o A) 4th century
- o B) **12th century**
- o C) Council of Nicaea
- o D) 1st century

What role does synergism play in theosis?

- o **A) Cooperation between divine grace and human effort**
- o B) God does all the work
- o C) Human effort alone saves
- o D) It only applies to monks and ascetics

Chapter 3:

Synergy—Cooperation Between Divine Grace and Human Effort

In Orthodox Christianity, the concept of **synergy**—the cooperation between **divine grace** and **human effort**—lies at the heart of the spiritual journey toward salvation. Unlike some traditions where salvation is viewed as a purely passive act of receiving God's grace, Orthodoxy teaches that we must actively participate in our salvation. This cooperation, or synergy, reflects a profound understanding of our relationship with God: while He initiates and sustains the process of salvation through His grace, we are called to respond with our will, actions, and efforts.

Synergy is not just a theological abstraction. It is lived out in the Christian life through prayer, fasting, ascetic practices, the veneration of **icons**, and participation in the **sacraments**. This dynamic cooperation between God's grace and human effort is essential for the journey toward **theosis**—the process of becoming more like God. This chapter explores the significance of synergy, the role of **asceticism**, and how icons aid prayer and spiritual growth.

The Story of St. Mary of Egypt — A Profound Example of Synergy

The life of **St. Mary of Egypt** provides a powerful illustration of synergy at work. Born in Egypt in the 5th century, Mary led a life of intense immorality for 17 years, indulging in worldly pleasures and leading others astray. However, her life took a dramatic turn when she attempted to enter the **Church of the Holy Sepulchre** in Jerusalem to venerate the **True Cross**. To her shock, an unseen force physically prevented her from crossing the threshold, and she suddenly realized that her sinful life was keeping her from entering the holy place.

Filled with remorse, she stood before an **icon of the Theotokos** (Mother of God) outside the church and prayed for forgiveness, vowing to change her ways. After this prayer, she was able to enter the church and venerate the Cross. This moment marked the beginning of her repentance. She fled to the desert beyond the Jordan River, where she spent the next 40 years in isolation, fasting, praying, and battling the temptations of her former life. Through her ascetic struggles and God's grace, Mary overcame her sins and was transformed into a great saint.

The story of St. Mary of Egypt illustrates the essence of synergy. **God's grace** led her to repentance by preventing her from entering the church, but it was her **response to that grace**—her decision to leave behind her sinful life and embrace a life of prayer and asceticism—that allowed her transformation to take place. Mary's story reminds us that while God provides the grace necessary for salvation, we must respond by actively cooperating with it through our own efforts. Her life shows how **asceticism**— the practice of self-denial and spiritual discipline—plays a crucial role in this process.

Theosis and Divine Grace: The Goal of Synergy

The ultimate goal of the Christian life, according to Orthodox theology, is **theosis**—the process by which human beings become partakers of the divine nature, as described in **2 Peter 1:4**: "He has granted to us His precious and very great promises, so that through them you may become partakers of the divine nature." Theosis is not simply about moral improvement or intellectual knowledge of God; it is about being transformed by God's **divine grace** into His likeness.

In Orthodox theology, grace is not understood as a created substance or external gift, but as the **uncreated energies of God**—His presence and activity in the world. These energies are what transform us, allowing us to participate in the divine life. Grace is essential for theosis, but grace alone is not enough. Synergy teaches that **human cooperation** with grace is necessary for it to bear fruit in our lives. We must freely choose to participate in the life of grace by aligning our will with God's will and engaging in practices that open our hearts to His transforming power.

This cooperation with grace is not a "work" that earns salvation, but rather a response to the gift of salvation. As **St. Paul** writes in **Philippians 2:12-13**, "Work out your own salvation with fear and trembling, for it is God who works in you, both to will and to work for His good pleasure." In other words, God provides the grace and strength, but we must "work out" our salvation through our choices, actions, and spiritual disciplines. This dynamic relationship between God's grace and human effort is what drives the process of theosis.

Asceticism: The Practice of Spiritual Discipline and Synergy

Asceticism—the practice of self-denial and spiritual discipline—is one of the primary ways that Orthodox Christians cooperate with God's grace. Asceticism involves practices such as fasting, prayer, almsgiving, and vigils, all of which help to purify the soul, overcome sinful passions, and focus the heart on God. The goal of asceticism is not simply to deny oneself for the sake of suffering, but to open oneself to the **transforming power of God's grace**.

Asceticism is an essential part of synergy because it requires active participation in the spiritual life. Through ascetic practices, we cooperate with God's grace by disciplining our bodies and minds and making room for His presence in our lives. The Orthodox Church teaches that our passions—such as anger, pride, gluttony, and lust—cloud our spiritual vision and prevent us from seeing God clearly. Through ascetic discipline, we can overcome these passions and create space for God's grace to work within us.

The **desert fathers and mothers** are exemplars of asceticism. One such figure is **St. Anthony the Great**, who is often called the father of monasticism. St. Anthony retreated to the desert to live a life of solitude, prayer, and fasting. In the desert, he faced intense spiritual warfare, battling temptations and demonic attacks. Yet through his ascetic practices, reliance on God's grace, and perseverance, he overcame these trials and became a model of holiness for future generations.

Asceticism also teaches us that spiritual growth is not instantaneous but requires time, effort, and patience. Just as a seed takes time to grow into a tree, so too does the spiritual life require continuous effort and nurturing.

Asceticism is the path by which we cooperate with grace to nurture the seed of faith and allow it to grow and bear fruit.

The Role of Icons in Prayer and Synergy

Icons hold a special place in Orthodox spirituality as **windows to heaven**—visible representations of spiritual realities that help lift our minds and hearts to God. Icons are not merely religious artwork or decoration; they are sacramental objects that point to the divine and provide a means of connecting with the **heavenly reality** they represent. Icons depict Christ, the **Theotokos**, the saints, and significant events in the life of the Church, reminding us of the ongoing presence of God and His saints in our lives.

Icons are also an important part of the **synergy** between divine grace and human effort. When we pray before an icon, we are not worshipping the image itself but venerating the holy person or event depicted in the icon. Through the icon, we enter into communion with the spiritual reality it represents. Icons help us focus our minds and hearts on God and inspire us to imitate the holiness of the saints.

For example, when we pray before an icon of **St. Mary of Egypt**, we are reminded of her repentance, ascetic struggle, and cooperation with God's grace. The icon serves as a visual aid that helps us focus our prayers and direct our thoughts toward God. By contemplating the life of St. Mary, we are encouraged to engage in our own spiritual struggles, trusting that God's grace will sustain us in our efforts.

Icons also remind us of the **Incarnation**, the foundational belief that God became man in the person of Jesus Christ. Because Christ took on human flesh, the material world is not seen as separate from the divine, but as capable of being **sanctified**. Icons reflect this truth by depicting Christ, the saints, and the events of salvation history in material form. By venerating icons, we acknowledge that the divine is present and active in the physical world, and that we, too, are called to become **living icons of Christ** through the process of theosis.

Icons aid in prayer by serving as focal points for contemplation and meditation. As we gaze upon an icon during prayer, we are reminded that the holy figures depicted in the icon are interceding for us and that their lives serve as examples of how to live in synergy with

God's grace. Icons help us to **lift our hearts and minds to God**, drawing us deeper into the spiritual life.

Spiritual Warfare and Synergy

An important aspect of synergy is the concept of **spiritual warfare**—the ongoing battle against the **passions, temptations,** and the forces of **evil** that seek to lead us away from God. The Christian life is not free from struggle; it is a constant battle to overcome sin and the distractions of the world. This spiritual warfare requires both **God's grace** and **our effort**.

In **Ephesians 6:12**, St. Paul writes, "For we do not wrestle against flesh and blood, but against the rulers, against the authorities, against the cosmic powers over this present darkness, against the spiritual forces of evil in the heavenly places." This battle is not fought with physical weapons but with prayer, fasting, vigilance, and reliance on God's grace. Spiritual warfare is where the synergy between divine grace and human effort becomes most evident.

In spiritual warfare, we cooperate with God's grace by resisting temptation, practicing **vigilance**, and striving to grow in virtue. Ascetic practices like fasting help to weaken the power of the passions, while prayer and the sacraments provide spiritual strength and nourishment. The grace of God sustains us in the struggle, but we must engage in the battle with perseverance and faith.

Conclusion: Synergy as the Path to Theosis

In Orthodox Christianity, **synergy**—the cooperation between divine grace and human effort—is the key to **theosis**, the process of becoming like God. While salvation is a gift of God's grace, we must actively participate in the process by responding with faith, repentance, and ascetic discipline. The lives of the saints, such as St. Mary of Egypt and St. Anthony the Great, show us that the path to holiness requires both divine empowerment and human struggle.

The **sacraments**, **ascetic practices**, and **icons** are all ways in which we engage in synergy, allowing God's grace to transform us into the likeness of Christ. Through this synergy, we are gradually conformed to the image of God, growing in holiness and union with Him.

CHAPTER 3. Concluding Prayer

O Lord Jesus Christ, who invites us to cooperate with Your divine grace, strengthen us in our spiritual struggles and guide us on the path of theosis. Help us to rely on Your grace while offering our efforts in prayer, repentance, and love. May we always strive to work out our salvation in cooperation with Your will, trusting in Your mercy and grace. For You are holy, now and ever, and unto ages of ages. Amen.

Chapter 3. Review Questions

What is synergy in Orthodox theology?

- o A) The work of God alone without human effort
- o B) The cooperation between divine grace and human effort
- o C) A theological concept that refers to prayer only
- o D) The belief that salvation is achieved solely by human works

What is theosis in Orthodox theology?

- o A) A state of moral perfection
- o B) The process of becoming like God and sharing in His divine nature
- o C) A theological idea about God's transcendence
- o D) A goal for monks and ascetics only

What is the purpose of asceticism in the Christian life?

- o A) To earn God's favor through self-denial
- o B) To discipline the body and soul, opening the heart to receive God's grace
- o C) To practice legalistic religious rules
- o D) To achieve a higher state of being

How do icons aid in the process of synergy?

- o A) By serving as windows to heaven, helping us focus on God and spiritual realities
- o B) By providing religious decoration for church walls
- o C) By being objects of worship in themselves
- o D) By offering historical depictions of saints

What is spiritual warfare in the context of synergy?

- o A) A battle fought only by monks
- o B) The constant struggle against sin and temptation, relying on both divine grace and human effort
- o C) A metaphor for reading the Bible regularly
- o D) An outdated concept no longer relevant to modern Christians

These review questions emphasize the dynamic cooperation between divine grace and human effort in the Orthodox Christian journey toward **theosis**, highlighting the essential role of asceticism, icons, and spiritual warfare in this synergy.

Chapter 4

The Role of the Sacraments in Salvation (Part 1)

In Orthodox Christianity, the sacraments—also known as the **Holy Mysteries**—are not mere rituals or symbolic gestures; they are the divinely ordained means by which we encounter God's grace and participate in the life of Christ. These sacraments are essential to our salvation because they enable us to grow in holiness, heal our souls, and experience the transformative power of God's grace. Orthodox theology teaches that salvation is not just about escaping punishment or entering heaven; it is about **theosis**—becoming more and more like God, sharing in His divine nature, and entering into eternal communion with Him.

This chapter explores the sacraments of **Baptism, Chrismation, Confession**, and the **Eucharist**, highlighting how these sacraments draw us closer to God, heal our souls, and strengthen us for the spiritual battle that is at the heart of the Christian life.

The Story of St. Nicholas and the Healing Power of Baptism

A beautiful example of the transformative power of Baptism can be found in the life of **St. Nicholas of Myra,** the 4th-century bishop renowned for his deep compassion and miraculous works. One day, a pagan family brought their gravely ill child to St. Nicholas, having heard of his reputation as a healer. The family, though not Christian, begged for his help, and St. Nicholas, moved by their plight, explained the power of **Baptism**—not only as a means of physical healing but as the gateway to eternal spiritual healing and life in Christ.

With the family's consent, St. Nicholas baptized the child in the name of the **Holy Trinity**. Almost immediately, the child's health began to improve, and within days, the child was completely restored. This miracle convinced the entire family to convert to Christianity, and they too were baptized by St. Nicholas.

This story illustrates the profound grace and healing found in the sacrament of **Baptism**. It is not merely a symbolic act but a real and transformative encounter with God's grace. Through Baptism, we are cleansed of sin, united with Christ in His death and resurrection, and initiated into the life of the Church. This is the first step on the path of **theosis**—the lifelong journey of becoming more like God.

Baptism — The Gateway to Theosis and the Beginning of the Spiritual Journey

In Orthodox theology, **Baptism** is often called the **gateway to salvation** because it is the sacrament through which we are united with Christ in His death and resurrection. The Apostle Paul speaks of this mystery in his letter to the Romans: "Do you not know that all of us who have been baptized into Christ Jesus were baptized into His death? We were buried therefore with Him by baptism into death, in order that, just as Christ was raised from the dead by the glory of the Father, we too might walk in newness of life" (**Romans 6:3-4**).

Through Baptism, we are **cleansed from sin**, including **Ancestral Sin** (the fallen condition inherited from Adam and Eve), and we are reborn into the life of grace. Baptism is not merely a symbolic gesture; it is a **sacramental reality** in which we are spiritually regenerated and made new. This sacrament marks the beginning of our journey toward **theosis**—the process of becoming more like God by sharing in His divine nature. As we grow in holiness, we draw closer to God and are gradually transformed into His likeness.

Theosis is the ultimate goal of the Christian life. It is not simply about moral improvement or outward behavior;

64

it is about an **inner transformation** by the grace of God. As St. Athanasius famously said, "God became man so that man might become god." This does not mean that we become gods by nature, but that we participate in God's divine life through His grace, growing in holiness and becoming more like Him in our love, humility, and righteousness. Baptism is the beginning of this transformative process, but it is just the first step. The grace received in Baptism must be nurtured and sustained through ongoing participation in the other sacraments, particularly **Confession** and the **Eucharist**.

Infant Baptism — The Grace of God Freely Given

Orthodox Christianity practices **infant baptism**, affirming that even the youngest members of the Church are in need of God's grace. Just as a child is born into a family without choosing it, so too are infants born into the family of God through Baptism. This practice highlights the truth that **salvation is a gift of grace** and not merely the result of our own efforts or decisions.

Some Protestant traditions reject infant baptism, arguing that a person must make a conscious decision to follow Christ before being baptized. However, the Orthodox Church teaches that **Baptism** is primarily about

God's action in our lives, not our own. It is a sacrament of grace, freely given to all who come to Christ, regardless of age or understanding. As the child grows, the grace of Baptism is nurtured and deepened through the support of parents, godparents, and the Church community.

The practice of infant baptism also underscores the communal nature of salvation in Orthodox theology. We are not saved in isolation but as members of the **Body of Christ**, the Church. The child is baptized into the Church, where they will be taught the faith, supported by the sacraments, and guided by the example of the saints and the faithful.

Chrismation — The Seal of the Holy Spirit and Empowerment for Spiritual Warfare

Immediately following Baptism, the newly baptized person receives the sacrament of **Chrismation**, which is the **seal of the gift of the Holy Spirit**. Chrismation is the Orthodox equivalent of **Confirmation** in the Western Christian tradition, and it completes the process of initiation into the Church. In this sacrament, the priest anoints the person with **holy chrism** (a special oil consecrated by the bishop), saying, "The seal of the gift of the Holy Spirit."

Just as the Apostles received the Holy Spirit on the day of **Pentecost**, empowering them to preach the Gospel and build the Church, so too does every Christian receive the Holy Spirit in **Chrismation**. The Holy Spirit equips us with spiritual gifts, strengthens us for the Christian life, and empowers us to engage in **spiritual warfare**—the ongoing battle against sin, temptation, and the forces of evil.

The grace of Chrismation is not a one-time event but a **continual source of strength** throughout the Christian life. It is the Holy Spirit who guides us, sanctifies us, and helps us grow in **theosis**. The gifts of the Holy Spirit, given in Chrismation, enable us to resist sin, grow in virtue, and fulfill our unique calling within the Body of Christ.

In the Orthodox understanding, the Christian life is a battle—a constant struggle against the passions, the devil, and the fallen world. This is where the concept of **spiritual warfare** comes in. The sacrament of Chrismation empowers us for this battle, arming us with the spiritual weapons needed to resist sin and grow in holiness. As St. Paul writes in **Ephesians 6:10-12**, "Finally, be strong in the Lord and in the strength of His might. Put on the whole armor of God, that you may be able to stand against the schemes of the devil. For we do not wrestle against flesh and blood, but against the rulers, against the authorities, against the cosmic powers over this present darkness, against the spiritual forces of evil in the heavenly places."

Confession — The Sacrament of Healing and Reconciliation

While Baptism cleanses us from all sin, the reality of human weakness means that we continue to struggle with sin throughout our lives. For this reason, the sacrament of **Confession**, or **Reconciliation**, is essential for the ongoing healing of the soul. In Orthodox Christianity, Confession is not just about admitting guilt or following legalistic rules; it is a **sacrament of healing**, where we encounter the **forgiveness** and **mercy** of God.

In **Confession**, the priest acts as a **living icon of Christ**, offering forgiveness and healing through the grace of the Holy Spirit. The priest does not forgive sins by his own power but acts as a vessel of God's mercy. This is a key distinction in Orthodox theology: the priest is not acting **in persona Christi** (in the person of Christ, as in Roman Catholic theology) but as a representative of the Church, through whom Christ Himself forgives and heals the penitent.

Confession is a sacrament of spiritual **renewal** and **restoration**. Every time we confess our sins with a contrite heart, we are cleansed, healed, and renewed by God's grace. St. John Chrysostom described Confession as a **second Baptism**, for through it, we are restored to the purity we received at Baptism. It is a sacrament of healing because it not only forgives our sins but also strengthens us to overcome them in the future.

The healing power of **Confession** is crucial to the process of **theosis**. As we confess our sins and receive God's forgiveness, the wounds caused by sin are healed, and we are made whole again. Confession helps us to grow in humility, making us more aware of our dependence on God's grace and our need for His mercy. This ongoing cycle of repentance, forgiveness, and renewal is central to the Christian life and is one of the primary means by which we grow in **theosis**.

The Eucharist — Ongoing Nourishment and the Source of Theosis

The **Eucharist** is the heart of Orthodox Christian life, and it is through this sacrament that we receive **ongoing nourishment** and **sanctification**. In the Divine Liturgy, the bread and wine are mystically transformed into the **Body and Blood of Christ**, and by partaking of Holy Communion, we are united with Christ in the most intimate way possible. As Jesus Himself said, "Truly, truly, I say to you, unless you eat the flesh of the Son of Man and drink His blood, you have no life in you" (**John 6:53**).

The Eucharist is not merely a symbolic remembrance of Christ's sacrifice; it is a **real participation** in His life-giving Body and Blood. Through the Eucharist, we receive the grace that sustains us on our journey of **theosis,** transforming us into the likeness of Christ. The Eucharist is the **sacrament of continual transformation**, drawing us ever closer to God and uniting us with the entire Body of Christ, the Church.

Each time we approach the chalice, we are renewed in our relationship with Christ and strengthened in our spiritual battle. The Eucharist cleanses us, heals us, and equips us to live out our Christian calling in the world. It is the **source and summit** of the Christian life, providing the grace that sustains all other aspects of our spiritual journey.

The Ongoing Role of the Sacraments in Salvation and Theosis

In Orthodox Christianity, salvation is not a one-time event but a **lifelong journey** of **theosis**—the process of becoming more like God. The sacraments are the **vehicles**

of grace that carry us along this path, continually renewing, healing, and transforming us.

- **Baptism** initiates us into the life of Christ, cleansing us from sin and uniting us with Him in His death and resurrection.
- **Chrismation** empowers us with the Holy Spirit, equipping us for the spiritual battle and helping us grow in holiness.
- **Confession** restores and heals us when we fall into sin, allowing us to be continually renewed in God's grace.
- **The Eucharist** nourishes and sanctifies us, drawing us deeper into communion with Christ and sustaining us on the journey of theosis.

The sacraments are not optional; they are essential for our salvation and spiritual growth. Through these Holy Mysteries, we participate in the divine life of Christ, growing in holiness and becoming more like Him. The sacraments provide the strength, healing, and nourishment we need to persevere in faith and ultimately attain eternal life in God's Kingdom.

CHAPTER 4. Concluding Prayer

O Lord Jesus Christ, who has given us the holy sacraments as the means of our salvation, grant that we may always approach them with reverence and faith. Through Baptism, Chrismation, Confession, and the Eucharist, may we be continually sanctified, healed, and transformed, growing ever closer to You. Strengthen us with Your grace and guide us on the path of theosis, that we may attain eternal life in Your Kingdom. For You are holy, now and ever, and unto ages of ages. Amen.

CHAPTER 4. Review Questions

What does Baptism accomplish in Orthodox Christianity?

- o A) It is a public declaration of faith
- o B) It cleanses us from sin and unites us with Christ's death and resurrection
- o C) It is a symbolic act of initiation into the Church
- o D) It only removes original sin

Why does the Orthodox Church practice infant baptism?

- A) Because infants are born into a sinful world
- B) Because Baptism is primarily about God's action in a person's life, not just a personal decision
- C) Because it is a tradition
- D) To give the child a Christian name

What is the role of Confession in Orthodox Christianity?

- A) It is a sacrament of healing and reconciliation, where we receive forgiveness for sins
- B) It is an optional spiritual practice
- C) It is a form of self-examination
- D) It is a ritual that has no lasting effect

What is the significance of the Eucharist in the life of an Orthodox Christian?

- o A) It is a symbolic meal
- o B) It is the real Body and Blood of Christ, providing ongoing spiritual nourishment and sanctification
- o C) It is only necessary for certain feast days
- o D) It is an act of remembrance only

Why is regular participation in the sacraments essential for Orthodox Christians?

- o A) Because they are religious obligations
- o B) Because they provide the grace necessary for salvation and spiritual growth
- o C) Because it is part of Orthodox tradition
- o D) Because it is a social expectation

These review questions deepen the understanding of how the sacraments—particularly Baptism, Chrismation, Confession, and the Eucharist—are essential for the lifelong journey of salvation and **theosis** in Orthodox Christianity.

Chapter 5

The Role of the Sacraments in Salvation (Part 2)

The life of **St. Paisios of Mount Athos**, one of the most revered modern saints of the Orthodox Church, offers a profound example of the central role the **sacraments** play in our journey to **salvation**. Born in 1924, St. Paisios lived a life of deep humility, love, and dedication to God. He was known for his spiritual wisdom and his ability to see into the hearts of those who came to him for advice and prayer. His teachings were always rooted in a deep reverence for the sacraments of the Church, especially the **Eucharist** and **Confession**.

One story from his life reveals how the sacraments are a continuous source of grace and renewal for the Christian soul. A man who had been away from the Church for many years came to St. Paisios, burdened by the weight of his sins and unsure if God would ever forgive him. He explained that he had lived a life far from God and felt that his soul was beyond redemption. St. Paisios, filled with compassion, encouraged the man to confess his sins to a priest and return to the Church.

After making a sincere **Confession**, the man attended the Divine Liturgy and received **Holy Communion** for the first time in years. He later returned to St. Paisios, filled with joy and peace, expressing how he felt as if a heavy burden had been lifted from his soul. St. Paisios reminded him that this was the transformative power of the sacraments—God's grace working to heal, forgive, and restore.

St. Paisios often spoke about the importance of continually participating in the sacraments, especially the Eucharist, as the nourishment for our souls. He compared the sacraments to medicine for the soul, explaining that just as we need regular food and medicine to maintain physical health, we need the sacraments to keep our spiritual life strong and to grow in holiness. Through the sacraments, the faithful receive the grace of God to help them along the path of **theosis**—the process of becoming more like God.

This story from the life of **St. Paisios** illustrates the importance of continually receiving the sacraments as the means by which we are sanctified and drawn closer to God. The sacraments are not optional rituals but essential encounters with God's grace that heal and transform us. Whether it is through **Confession** and the **Eucharist**, or through other sacraments like **Holy Unction** or **Holy Matrimony**, these sacred mysteries are the way in which God's grace becomes active in our lives, leading us on the path to salvation.

In Orthodox Christianity, the sacraments are essential means of grace that allow us to participate in the life of Christ and experience the fullness of our salvation. These sacraments are not symbolic rituals but real encounters with God, where we are transformed by His divine grace. The sacraments are an expression of our deep relationship with Christ and the Church, and they are essential to our spiritual growth and theosis—the process of becoming more like God. In the previous chapter, we discussed Baptism and Chrismation as sacraments of initiation, marking the beginning of the Christian life. In this chapter, we explore the ongoing role of the Eucharist and Confession in sustaining our relationship with God, as well as the Orthodox understanding of grace and the practice of infant Baptism and Chrismation.

A key contrast between Orthodox Christianity and many Evangelical Protestant traditions lies in the understanding of a personal relationship with Jesus. While Protestants often emphasize a direct, individual connection with Christ based on a profession of faith, Orthodox Christianity teaches that our relationship with Christ is lived out most fully in the sacraments, particularly in the

Eucharist, where we encounter Christ in His real presence. Unfortunately, many Protestant Christians reject this real presence, which mirrors the reaction of some of Jesus' followers in John 6, who turned away from Him after hearing His teaching about the Bread of Life.

In this chapter, we will also contrast the Orthodox sacrament of Chrismation with the Roman Catholic sacrament of Confirmation, as well as explain why the Orthodox Church practices infant Baptism and Chrismation, rather than relying on a profession of faith later in life, as many Protestant churches do.

The Orthodox Understanding of Grace

To understand the sacraments and their role in salvation, it is crucial to grasp the Orthodox understanding of grace. In Orthodox theology, grace is not merely an external favor that God bestows upon us. It is not an abstract concept or a legal declaration of righteousness, as some Protestant traditions might teach. Rather, grace is the uncreated energy of God—the actual presence and power of God at work in our lives. Grace is the life of God given to us so that we might be transformed and participate in His divine nature.

As the Apostle Peter writes, "He has granted to us His precious and very great promises, so that through them you may become partakers of the divine nature" (2 Peter 1:4). This participation in the divine nature is made possible through the grace of God, which is imparted to us in the sacraments. Each sacrament is a unique encounter with God's grace, a moment when His divine life flows into us and transforms us from within.

In this understanding, grace is not something we can earn or merit. It is a free gift from God, but it requires our cooperation—our synergy with God's work. The sacraments, then, are the means by which we receive and cooperate with this divine grace. They are not human works but divine actions, in which God makes Himself present to us and draws us into communion with Him.

Chrismation: Empowerment by the Holy Spirit

Following Baptism, the Orthodox Christian is immediately anointed with holy chrism in the sacrament of Chrismation. Chrismation is the sacrament through which the newly baptized Christian receives the seal of the Holy Spirit, empowering them to live a life of faith and holiness. The priest anoints various parts of the body with holy chrism, saying, "The seal of the gift of the Holy Spirit."

This anointing is a real, sacramental action through which the Holy Spirit is given to the believer, strengthening them for the Christian life.

St. Cyril of Jerusalem emphasizes the importance of Chrismation, saying, "You have become Christ-bearers by receiving the seal of the Holy Spirit." This sacrament is not merely symbolic; it is a real encounter with the Holy Spirit, who fills the Christian with grace and equips them to resist sin, grow in virtue, and live out their faith in the world.

While Chrismation is similar to the Roman Catholic sacrament of Confirmation, there are important differences between the two. In the Roman Catholic tradition, Confirmation is often delayed until adolescence or adulthood and is seen as a sacrament of maturity and commitment to the faith. In the Orthodox Church, however, Chrismation is administered immediately after Baptism, even to infants, because it is understood as part of the Christian's initiation into the life of the Church. Chrismation is not about reaching a certain level of maturity but about receiving the Holy Spirit, who empowers the Christian from the very beginning of their spiritual journey.

The Eucharist: The Real Presence of Christ

The Eucharist is the central sacrament of the Orthodox Church and the ultimate expression of our relationship with Christ. In the Eucharist, we receive the Body and Blood of Christ, not symbolically but truly and really. The bread and wine, through the mystery of the Eucharist, become the real presence of Christ, given to us for the forgiveness of sins and eternal life. The Eucharist is not merely a memorial of Christ's sacrifice; it is the actual participation in His death and resurrection, by which we are united with Him.

Jesus Himself instituted the Eucharist during the Last Supper, saying, "Take, eat; this is My body... Drink of it, all of you, for this is My blood of the covenant, which is poured out for many for the forgiveness of sins" (Matthew 26:26-28). He makes the necessity of the Eucharist clear in John 6, where He says, "Truly, truly, I say to you, unless you eat the flesh of the Son of Man and drink His blood, you have no life in you" (John 6:53).

The Eucharist is essential for our spiritual life because, through it, we receive the life of Christ into our own bodies and souls. St. Ignatius of Antioch called the Eucharist the "medicine of immortality," for through it we are nourished and sustained on our journey toward theosis. The Eucharist is the most intimate and transformative encounter with

Christ, for in receiving His Body and Blood, we are united with Him in a way that goes beyond intellectual belief or emotional experience. This union with Christ in the Eucharist is the fullest expression of our personal relationship with Him.

Protestant Rejection of the Real Presence: A Parallel to John 6:66

Many Protestant Christians, particularly in Evangelical traditions, reject the idea of the real presence of Christ in the Eucharist. They view the Eucharist as a symbolic act, a memorial of Christ's death rather than a real participation in His Body and Blood. This rejection of the real presence mirrors the reaction of some of Jesus' followers in John 6, who could not accept His teaching about the necessity of eating His flesh and drinking His blood.

In John 6:66, we read, "After this many of His disciples turned back and no longer walked with Him." These disciples found Jesus' teaching too difficult to accept, and they chose to turn away rather than embrace the mystery of the Eucharist. Unfortunately, many Protestant Christians today repeat this response by rejecting the mystical reality of the Eucharist, favoring a more symbolic interpretation that is easier to grasp.

Orthodox Christians, by contrast, embrace the mystery of the Eucharist. We believe that the bread and wine truly become the Body and Blood of Christ, and that by receiving the Eucharist, we are united with Him in the most intimate and transformative way possible. The Eucharist is not just a symbol; it is the real, living presence of Christ, and through this sacrament, we receive the grace to continue our journey toward salvation and theosis.

Confession: Healing and Restoring Communion

While the Eucharist sustains our relationship with Christ, the sacrament of Confession heals and restores that relationship when it is damaged by sin. Sin creates a separation between us and God, and through Confession, we receive the grace of forgiveness and are reconciled with Christ and the Church.

In 1 John 1:9, we read, "If we confess our sins, He is faithful and just to forgive us our sins and to cleanse us from all unrighteousness." Confession is not simply about admitting guilt; it is about repentance—a turning away from sin and a turning back to God. Through Confession, we are cleansed of our sins and restored to full communion with Christ, allowing us to approach the Eucharist with a pure heart and a clean conscience.

The priest, acting as a representative of Christ, hears our confession and grants absolution in the name of the Church. As St. John Chrysostom reminds us, "It is not the priest who forgives sin, but God who forgives through the priest." Confession is a sacrament of healing, through which we experience the mercy of God and are renewed in His grace.

The Practice of Infant Baptism and Chrismation

One of the key differences between Orthodox Christianity and many Protestant traditions is the practice of infant Baptism and Chrismation. In many Protestant churches, particularly in Baptist and Evangelical circles, Baptism is reserved for those who are old enough to make a profession of faith. This practice, often called "believer's Baptism," is based on the idea that faith is a personal decision, and only those who can consciously choose to follow Christ should be baptized.

In the Orthodox Church, however, infant Baptism and Chrismation are practiced because the sacraments are seen as the means by which we receive God's grace, not as rewards for our personal decision. In Orthodox theology, Baptism is the sacrament that initiates us into the life of Christ and the Church, and it is not dependent on our intellectual understanding or personal decision. Infants are baptized because they, too, need the grace of God and the cleansing of original sin. As Jesus said, "Let the little children come to Me, and do not hinder them, for to such belongs the kingdom of God" (Mark 10:14).

The Orthodox Church understands that grace is a free gift from God, given to all, regardless of age or intellectual capacity. Infant Baptism and Chrismation emphasize that it is God who initiates the relationship with us, not the other way around. Faith is important, but it is something that grows and matures throughout our life as we respond to God's grace. By baptizing infants, the Church ensures that they are initiated into the Christian life from the very beginning, receiving the grace of the Holy Spirit through Chrismation and being nourished by the sacraments as they grow in faith.

Chapter 5. Concluding Prayer

O Lord Jesus Christ, who gave us the sacraments as gifts of Your grace and means of communion with You, grant us the grace to receive them with faith and reverence. Strengthen us through the power of Your Holy Spirit, poured out in Chrismation, and nourish us through Your Body and Blood in the Eucharist. Heal us through the sacrament of Confession, that we may be restored to full communion with You. Help us to embrace the mystery of Your real presence and to live in the fullness of Your grace, both now and forever. Amen.

Chapter 5. Review Questions
What is the Orthodox understanding of grace?

A) It is a legal declaration of righteousness

B) It is the uncreated energy of God, given to us so we can participate in His divine life

C) It is something we can earn through good works

D) It is an abstract concept with no real effect on our lives

What is the role of Chrismation in Orthodox Christianity?

A) It is a symbolic act of confirming one's faith

B) It is the sealing of the Holy Spirit, empowering the Christian for a life of faith

C) It is an optional rite for mature Christians

D) It is a repeat of Baptism

Why does the Orthodox Church practice infant Baptism and Chrismation?

A) Because infants do not need a personal profession of faith

B) Because God's grace is a free gift that does not depend on age or intellectual capacity

C) Because Baptism should only be given to those who are mature in their faith

D) Because infants are incapable of sin

What does Jesus teach about the Eucharist in John 6?

A) It is a symbolic remembrance of His death

B) It is not necessary for salvation

C) Unless you eat His flesh and drink His blood, you have no life in you

D) It is a private act of devotion

How does Confession restore our relationship with Christ?

A) By allowing us to admit our sins publicly

B) By cleansing us of sin and reconciling us with Christ and the Church

C) By removing the need for the Eucharist

D) By making us feel better about our mistakes

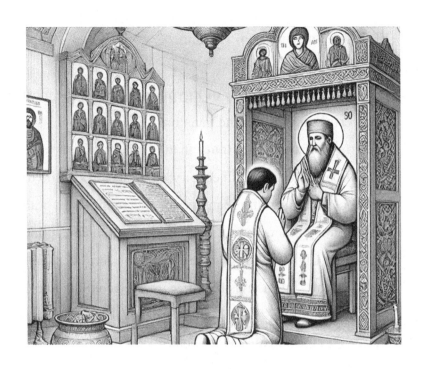

Chapter 6

Confession and Repentance

The Sacrament of Healing

The life of St. Mary of Egypt offers one of the most powerful examples of the transformative power of **Confession** and **Repentance** in the Orthodox Christian tradition. Born in the 5th century, St. Mary lived a life of extreme sinfulness for many years, engaging in immorality and leading others astray. Yet, one day, while attempting to enter the Church of the Holy Sepulchre in Jerusalem, she was stopped by an invisible force. Stricken with remorse for her sinful life, she fell to her knees in repentance and prayed to the **Theotokos** for help.

After receiving forgiveness through her sincere repentance, Mary fled into the desert, where she spent the next 47 years in solitude, fasting, praying, and doing penance for her past sins. Through her life of deep repentance, she achieved great holiness, and her soul was purified by God's grace. Her encounter with **St. Zosimas**, a priest-monk who heard her confession and gave her Holy Communion before she passed away, demonstrates the beauty of how God's forgiveness works through the sacraments, offering us healing and reconciliation with Him.

The story of St. Mary of Egypt reminds us that no matter how far we may stray from God, there is always a path back to Him through **repentance** and **confession**. The sacrament of Confession is a sacred opportunity to be reconciled with God and the Church, to receive His healing grace, and to begin anew in the journey toward salvation.

The story of **St. Mary of Egypt** illustrates the profound healing that comes through the sacrament of **Confession**. Just as she experienced God's mercy and forgiveness after years of living in sin, so too are we offered the opportunity for spiritual healing through this holy sacrament. Confession is a sacrament of **healing** because it restores our relationship with God, cleanses our souls from the burden of sin, and helps us grow in holiness.

This chapter explores the role of Confession and repentance in Orthodox Christianity, explaining how this sacrament helps us to be reconciled with God, receive His grace, and heal from the wounds caused by sin. It also contrasts Orthodox views on Confession with other Christian traditions, emphasizing the unique sacramental nature of this path to spiritual healing.

In Orthodox Christianity, the sacraments are the lifelines through which we experience God's grace. They are not symbolic gestures, but real, tangible encounters with the Divine. Among these sacraments, **Confession** (or **Reconciliation**) plays a crucial role as a means of **healing** and **spiritual restoration**. Through the sacrament of Confession, we are reconciled with God, healed from the effects of sin, and restored to our place in the Church community. However, this healing requires our sincere participation in **repentance**—the lifelong process of turning away from sin and back toward God.

This chapter explores the sacrament of Confession from an Orthodox perspective, discussing its role in spiritual healing, the importance of repentance, and how these concepts differ from certain **Protestant** practices of confession. We will also contrast the Orthodox understanding of the priest's role in Confession—where the priest serves as a **living icon of Christ**—with the **Roman Catholic** idea of the priest acting **in persona Christi** (in the person of Christ). This distinction highlights important theological nuances in how both traditions view the function of the priesthood in the sacramental life of the Church.

Repentance: A Continuous Journey Toward God

In Orthodox Christianity, **repentance** is not a one-time event or a fleeting emotion. It is an ongoing process, a daily turning of the heart and mind toward God. The Greek word for repentance, *metanoia*, means "a change of mind." This transformation involves acknowledging our sins, turning away from them, and reorienting our lives toward God's will. Repentance is an integral part of Christian life because it reflects the constant struggle to overcome our passions, selfishness, and the spiritual forces that lead us away from God.

St. John Climacus, in his classic spiritual text *The Ladder of Divine Ascent*, calls repentance "the renewal of baptism" and "a contract with God for a fresh start in life." Repentance allows us to return to the grace we received at Baptism, re-committing ourselves to the path of holiness. It is not just for grievous sins, but for the smaller, everyday sins that weigh down our spiritual life. Without regular repentance, these sins can accumulate and distance us from God.

Repentance is not only about feeling sorry for what we have done. Rather, it is about genuinely **turning away from sin** and striving to live in a way that aligns with the teachings of Christ. This process is lifelong, as we constantly strive to become more like God and grow in holiness. Confession, as the sacrament of healing, allows us to **articulate** our repentance, bringing our sins before God through the **living icon of Christ**, the priest.

The Sacrament of Confession: Healing Through Grace

In Orthodox Christianity, Confession is not merely about admitting guilt; it is about experiencing **healing** through the forgiveness of sins. Sin is understood as a **spiritual illness**, something that not only breaks God's commandments but also harms our relationship with Him, others, and ourselves. Just as physical illnesses require treatment, so too do the spiritual wounds caused by sin require healing. The sacrament of Confession is the means by which these wounds are treated, allowing us to be restored to **spiritual health**.

In **James 5:16**, we are told to "confess your sins to one another and pray for one another, that you may be healed." Confession is a sacrament of **healing**—it is through Confession that we receive the grace of forgiveness, which heals the damage that sin causes in our souls. By confessing our sins and receiving absolution, we are reconciled with God, the Church, and ourselves.

The priest, in hearing the confession and offering absolution, acts not as a personal judge or intermediary but as a **living icon of Christ**. This distinction is important. In Roman Catholicism, the priest acts **in persona Christi**—literally "in the person of Christ"—which means that during the sacraments, the priest stands as Christ Himself, performing the sacrament on behalf of Christ. In contrast, in the Orthodox Church, the priest does not **become** Christ in a juridical sense but represents Him as a **living icon**. The priest is a witness to the penitent's confession and serves as a conduit through which God's grace flows, but the forgiveness comes from Christ Himself, not from the priest.

As **St. John Chrysostom** writes, "The priest only lends his tongue and hands, but it is God who forgives." This idea emphasizes that the priest, as a living icon, facilitates the sacrament, but the action and authority belong entirely to God. The priest's role is one of service and humility, standing in as a representative of the Church while guiding the penitent back to Christ's healing love.

The Healing Power of Confession: A Fresh Start

One of the most beautiful aspects of the sacrament of Confession is that it offers a **fresh start**. No matter what sins we have committed, no matter how far we have strayed from God, His mercy is always available to us. **Psalm 103:12** assures us, "As far as the east is from the west, so far does He remove our transgressions from us." Through Confession, our sins are not only forgiven but also **removed**, and we are given the grace to begin again.

Confession is a sacrament of **peace** and **renewal**. Carrying the burden of sin can be spiritually and emotionally draining, but through Confession, we experience God's healing grace, which lifts that burden and restores our inner peace. We are not left alone to struggle with guilt; rather, God gives us the assurance of His forgiveness through the words of the priest: "May God, through me, a sinner, forgive you." This assurance brings a deep sense of peace and healing, allowing us to move forward on our spiritual journey with a renewed sense of purpose and clarity.

Contrasting Protestant and Orthodox Views of Confession

The practice of Confession is one of the significant theological differences between **Orthodox Christianity** and **Protestantism**. In many Protestant traditions, especially in **Evangelical** and **Reformed** circles, there is no sacrament of Confession to a priest. Instead, confession of sins is typically seen as a personal, private matter between the individual and God. Protestants often emphasize the **priesthood of all believers**, believing that every Christian has direct access to God and that there is no need for a priestly intermediary.

This difference stems from the **Reformation**, during which figures like **Martin Luther** rejected the authority of the priesthood and the practice of sacramental Confession. Protestants generally believe that forgiveness can be obtained through personal repentance and prayer, without the need for sacramental absolution. The Protestant understanding of Confession is therefore more focused on the individual's direct relationship with God, with less emphasis on the role of the Church or the clergy.

In contrast, Orthodox Christianity sees the sacrament of Confession as essential for spiritual healing and restoration. The priest is not an intermediary who stands between the penitent and God, but a **living icon of Christ**—a witness to the confession who offers absolution in Christ's name. The words of absolution spoken by the priest are not his own; they are the words of Christ, spoken through the priest by the authority of the Church. This sacramental act provides the penitent with the **assurance of forgiveness**, something that is often lacking in purely private confession.

Orthodox theology also emphasizes the **communal** nature of Confession. While the act of confessing is personal, it takes place within the context of the Church, which is the Body of Christ. When we sin, we not only damage our relationship with God but also with the Church community. Through sacramental Confession, we are reconciled both to God and to the Church. This is why Confession is often referred to as the **sacrament of reconciliation**—it restores the penitent to communion with both God and the Church.

Repentance: The Foundation of Spiritual Growth

In Orthodox Christianity, **repentance** is not only about admitting guilt but also about **spiritual transformation**. It is the foundation of **spiritual growth** and is necessary for deepening our relationship with God. As we grow in our faith, we become more aware of our sins and our need for

God's grace. Repentance is how we continually turn back to God, realigning our lives with His will.

Repentance is a lifelong process because the Christian life is a journey toward **theosis**—the process of becoming more like God. As we strive to grow in holiness, we are constantly confronted with our weaknesses and failures. Yet, repentance is not meant to lead us into despair but into **humility** and deeper reliance on God's grace. **St. Isaac the Syrian** reminds us, "This life has been given to you for repentance. Do not waste it on vain pursuits." Repentance, then, is the key to spiritual renewal and growth.

The Priest as a Living Icon of Christ

The role of the priest in the sacrament of Confession is unique in Orthodox theology. While Roman Catholicism holds that the priest acts **in persona Christi**—in the person of Christ—Orthodox Christianity teaches that the priest is a **living icon of Christ**. This distinction reflects different theological emphases regarding the priesthood.

In the Roman Catholic view, when the priest administers a sacrament, he is believed to be standing in for Christ, acting with Christ's authority as His representative. This understanding is rooted in the idea that the priest, during the administration of the sacraments, takes on a **juridical** role in offering Christ's grace.

In the Orthodox Church, the priest serves as a **living icon**—he represents Christ, but he does not take on Christ's person in a juridical sense. The priest remains fully human and a servant of the Church. He stands before the penitent as a visible reminder of Christ's presence and serves as a conduit for God's grace, but it is ultimately Christ who forgives and heals. The priest, therefore, facilitates the sacrament by offering absolution in Christ's name, but the act of forgiveness comes from God alone.

This theology highlights the Orthodox understanding of the priesthood as a **pastoral** and **humble** role. The priest does not wield authority in and of himself but serves the Church and the faithful as a minister of God's grace. The priest, as a **living icon**, points the penitent to Christ, guiding them back into communion with God and the Church through the sacrament of Confession.

Chapter 6. Concluding Prayer

O Lord Jesus Christ, who in Your infinite mercy forgives all those who repent and turn to You, grant us the grace to confess our sins with humility and sincerity. May Your priest, as a living icon of Your presence, guide us toward reconciliation and healing. Help us to turn away from sin and to walk the path of repentance, that we may be renewed by Your grace and restored to full communion with You. For You are the Physician of our souls, and to You we give glory, together with the Father and the Holy Spirit, now and ever and unto ages of ages. Amen.

Chapter 6. Review Questions

What is the meaning of repentance in Orthodox Christianity?

- o A) Feeling guilty for sins
- o B) A complete change of heart and mind, turning away from sin and toward God
- o C) A one-time emotional experience
- o D) A public confession of wrongdoing

What role does the priest play in Orthodox Confession?

- o A) The priest acts as an intermediary between the penitent and God
- o B) The priest acts as a living icon of Christ, witnessing the confession and offering absolution in Christ's name

o C) The priest personally forgives the sins of the penitent

o D) The priest determines whether the penitent's sins can be forgiven

How does Orthodox Christianity differ from Roman Catholicism in its understanding of the priest's role in the sacraments?

o A) In Orthodoxy, the priest acts in persona Christi (in the person of Christ)

o B) In Orthodoxy, the priest serves as a living icon of Christ, not as a substitute for Him

o C) In Orthodoxy, the priest has no role in sacramental Confession

o D) In Roman Catholicism, the priest does not represent Christ in any way

Why is Confession important for spiritual healing in Orthodox Christianity?

o A) It is a legal obligation to the Church

o B) It offers forgiveness and healing for the soul, restoring the individual's relationship with God and the Church

o C) It is a way to avoid punishment for sins

- D) It is optional for those who feel particularly guilty

What is the purpose of sacramental absolution in Orthodox Confession?

- A) It serves as a reminder of God's mercy
- B) It provides assurance that the penitent's sins are forgiven by Christ through the Church
- C) It only applies to serious sins
- D) It allows the priest to impose a punishment on the penitent

Chapter 7

Holy Matrimony

A Sacrament of Union and a Path to Salvation

The Sacrament of Marriage in Orthodox Christianity

The life of **Sts. Peter and Febronia of Murom**, often regarded as the patron saints of married couples in Orthodox Christianity, provides a beautiful example of the sacrament of **Holy Matrimony** as a path to salvation. Living in 13th-century Russia, Peter was a prince who ruled over the city of Murom, and Febronia was a humble peasant woman known for her deep faith and wisdom. Their marriage was marked by a profound love, mutual respect, and devotion to God, qualities that defined their relationship.

Before they married, Prince Peter became gravely ill with a mysterious disease that no one could cure. Hearing of Febronia's spiritual wisdom, he sought her help. Febronia not only healed him through her prayers but also impressed him with her humility and piety. Despite opposition from his royal court, Peter chose to marry Febronia, recognizing that their union was rooted in their shared faith and commitment to God.

Their marriage was not without challenges. Many of the nobles in Peter's court disapproved of their union and plotted against them. At one point, they were forced into exile, stripped of their royal privileges. Yet, through it all, Peter and Febronia remained united in their love for each other and their trust in God. They supported one another, prayed together, and faced their trials with patience and humility.

Eventually, the people of Murom realized their mistake and begged the couple to return and rule over them once again. Peter and Febronia returned, governing with wisdom and compassion. They lived out their days in peace, and when the time came for them to depart this life, they both entered monastic life and died on the same day, in adjoining cells, symbolizing their unbreakable bond even in death.

Their story is a powerful example of how the sacrament of Holy Matrimony is a **path to salvation**. Through their love for one another and their steadfast commitment to God, Peter and Febronia became saints, showing that marriage is not just about personal happiness but about growing in holiness together.

The story of **Sts. Peter and Febronia** illustrates the sacramental nature of marriage in Orthodox Christianity.

Their union, like all Christian marriages, was a reflection of the love between **Christ and the Church**—a love that is selfless, sacrificial, and sanctifying. Their lives demonstrate that through the challenges and joys of marriage, couples are called to grow in their faith, support one another on the path to salvation, and ultimately find their true union in God's eternal Kingdom.

This story highlights the importance of the sacrament of Holy Matrimony as a **means of grace** and a path to holiness, where husband and wife are called to help each other grow closer to God through their love and mutual sacrifice.

In Orthodox Christianity, marriage is much more than a civil institution or a contract. It is a sacred and sacramental union that mirrors Christ's love for the Church and serves as a path toward salvation. The sacrament of Holy Matrimony unites a man and a woman into one flesh (Ephesians 5:31-32), empowering them through divine grace to journey together toward theosis—the process of becoming more like God. Marriage in the Orthodox Church is fundamentally about love, sacrifice, and mutual sanctification, with the couple helping one another along the road to salvation.

In this chapter, we will examine the Orthodox understanding of marriage, its sacramental nature, and the spiritual responsibilities it entails. We will also contrast Orthodox views of marriage with secular and Protestant perspectives, some of which focus on marriage more as a social contract or personal covenant than as a means of receiving God's grace.

Marriage as a Sacrament: A Holy Mystery

In Orthodox Christianity, marriage is one of the seven sacraments (also known as holy mysteries), meaning that it is a sacred act through which divine grace is conferred. The sacrament of marriage reflects the mystical union of Christ and His Church, as described by St. Paul in Ephesians 5:25: "Husbands, love your wives, as Christ loved the Church and gave Himself up for her." This self-sacrificial love serves as the model for Christian marriage. It is through this love that husband and wife grow in holiness, becoming icons of Christ and His bride, the Church.

The Orthodox wedding ceremony beautifully illustrates the sacramental nature of marriage, particularly through the crowning ceremony. During this part of the service, the bride and groom are crowned with ceremonial crowns that symbolize not only their union as king and queen of their household but also the martyrdom of self-sacrifice that each spouse is called to embrace. Just as Christ laid down His life for the Church, the husband and wife are called to lay down their lives for one another in love and service.

Marriage in Orthodoxy is therefore not just a partnership or a mutual agreement but a mystical participation in the love of God. The sacrament of marriage consecrates the natural bond between husband and wife, infusing it with divine grace, which strengthens and sanctifies the couple, enabling them to grow in their love for one another and for God.

Marriage as a Path to Salvation

In the Orthodox Church, marriage is understood as a pathway to salvation. The goal of Christian life is theosis—becoming more like God—and marriage provides a unique context in which two people can pursue this together. Through the sacrament of marriage, the husband and wife are called to help each other grow spiritually, to bear one another's burdens, and to walk together in their journey toward eternal life.

This understanding of marriage as a path to salvation is rooted in the concept of synergy—the cooperation between human effort and divine grace. The husband and wife, by striving to live out their marriage in love, humility, and self-sacrifice, participate in God's work of salvation. Their mutual love and service are not merely a reflection of human affection but a means by which they are drawn closer to God and conformed to the image of Christ.

St. John Chrysostom, a great teacher of the Church, wrote extensively about the sanctifying nature of marriage. He taught that the love between husband and wife is a reflection of Christ's love for the Church, and through this love, the couple can help each other attain salvation. Marriage, in this view, is not an end in itself but a means of growing in holiness and leading one another toward eternal life.

The Spiritual Responsibilities of Marriage

Marriage in the Orthodox tradition comes with significant spiritual responsibilities. The husband and wife are called to support one another not only in the material and emotional aspects of life but also in their spiritual growth. This includes:

Praying together: Couples are encouraged to pray together regularly, both at home and during church services.

Attending the sacraments together: Regular participation in the sacraments, particularly the Eucharist, strengthens the bond of marriage and nourishes the couple's spiritual life.

Fostering forgiveness: One of the key responsibilities of marriage is to practice forgiveness. Disagreements and conflicts are inevitable, but the grace of marriage enables the couple to forgive one another and grow through their struggles.

Orthodox Christianity teaches that the family is a domestic church—a small church within the home, where the husband and wife serve as spiritual leaders. In this role, they are responsible for raising their children in the faith, teaching them to love God, and setting an example of Christian virtue. The sacramental grace of marriage gives parents the strength to fulfill these responsibilities, helping them to create a home where Christ is present and His love is reflected in the daily life of the family.

Sacramental Grace in Marriage

The sacrament of Holy Matrimony imparts sacramental grace to the couple, enabling them to live out their marriage in a way that reflects the love of Christ for the Church. This grace is essential for overcoming the challenges and difficulties that arise in married life. Without it, marriage can easily become focused on self-interest or personal fulfillment. With it, marriage becomes a path of self-sacrificial love, where each spouse seeks to serve the other and grow in holiness together.

St. Gregory the Theologian emphasized the importance of sacramental grace in marriage, teaching that it is through this grace that the couple's natural love is sanctified and transformed into a reflection of God's divine love. This grace strengthens the couple's commitment to one another and enables them to persevere in love even in the face of hardship.

Sacramental grace also plays a key role in the procreative aspect of marriage. In Orthodox Christianity, children are seen as a blessing from God, and the grace of marriage helps the couple raise their children in the faith. The sacramental life of the Church provides the family with the spiritual tools they need to grow together in love and holiness.

Contrasting Secular and Protestant Views of Marriage

In secular society, marriage is often viewed primarily as a contract between two individuals, based on mutual love and personal fulfillment. In this view, marriage is often approached with an emphasis on individual happiness and self-interest. If a marriage no longer meets the needs or desires of one or both partners, it is often seen as something that can be dissolved through divorce. While secular marriage may emphasize companionship and personal growth, it generally lacks the sacramental dimension found in Orthodox Christianity.

In certain Protestant traditions, marriage is viewed as a covenant between two people and God, but it may not be understood as a sacrament in the same way it is in Orthodoxy or Roman Catholicism. For many Protestants, marriage is seen as a solemn commitment, but it is often viewed more as a human institution than a divine mystery. The idea of sacramental grace is not always emphasized, and marriage may be seen primarily as a personal relationship rather than as a means of participating in God's work of salvation.

In contrast, the Orthodox Church teaches that marriage is a sacrament that imparts real grace to the couple, enabling them to live out their marriage in a way that leads them to salvation. Marriage in Orthodoxy is not simply a human contract or a personal relationship; it is a holy mystery through which the couple is united by God and sanctified by His grace. Divorce, while sometimes permitted for reasons such as adultery or abuse, is seen as a tragic failure to live up to the sacramental calling of marriage. The Church encourages couples to seek reconciliation and healing through the grace of God before considering divorce.

The Role of Children and the Domestic Church

In Orthodox Christianity, children are viewed as a blessing from God and an integral part of the marital union. The family is seen as a domestic church, where the husband and wife are called to create a spiritual environment in which their children can grow in faith and love for God. The sacrament of marriage gives the couple the grace to fulfill this sacred responsibility, helping them to teach their children the Christian virtues of love, humility, and forgiveness.

Parents, through the grace of Holy Matrimony, are called to be spiritual guides for their children, helping them to understand the faith and live according to Christ's commandments. In this way, the family becomes a small church, where Christ is present and where the faith is nurtured.

Chapter 7. Concluding Prayer

O Lord Jesus Christ, who blessed the wedding at Cana and sanctified the union of husband and wife, bless all those who are united in the sacrament of Holy Matrimony. Grant them the grace to love one another with the self-sacrificial love that You have for Your Church. Strengthen them in their union, help them to forgive one another, and guide them on the path to salvation. For You are the source of all love, and to You we give glory, together with the Father and the Holy Spirit, now and ever and unto ages of ages. Amen.

Chapter 7. Review Questions

What is the primary purpose of marriage in Orthodox Christianity?

A) Personal happiness and fulfillment

B) Procreation

C) Growing in holiness and leading each other

toward salvation

D) Mutual convenience

What does the crowning ceremony in Orthodox weddings symbolize?

A) The couple's financial success

B) The couple's role as king and queen of their household, and their calling to sacrificial love

C) The public recognition of their marriage

D) Their social status in the community

What is the significance of sacramental grace in Orthodox marriage?

A) It strengthens the couple in their commitment and helps them live out their marriage as a path to holiness

B) It is not important in modern marriage

C) It is only given to couples who never argue

D) It is optional and depends on individual merit

What is the role of parents in the domestic church?

A) To maintain household finances

B) To raise their children in the faith and create a home where Christ is central

C) To focus on their children's worldly success

D) To keep the family traditions without concern for spiritual growth

How does the Orthodox Church view divorce?

A) It is always encouraged if personal happiness is not achieved

B) It is sometimes permitted for reasons such as adultery or abuse, but is seen as a tragic failure to live up to the sacramental calling of marriage

C) It is forbidden under all circumstances

D) It is not relevant to modern relationships

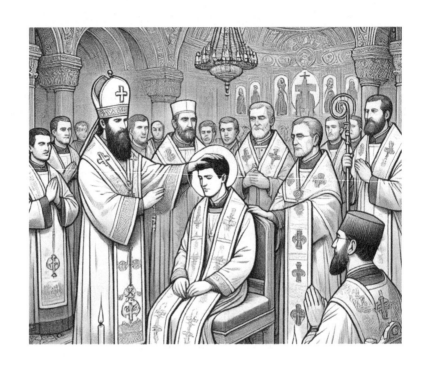

Chapter 8

Holy Orders—The Sacrament of Apostolic Ministry

The Role of Holy Orders in the Life of the Church

The life of **St. Nektarios of Aegina** offers a remarkable example of the grace and power imparted through the sacrament of **Holy Orders**. St. Nektarios was a bishop who faced great trials and persecution throughout his ministry, often slandered and falsely accused by jealous contemporaries. Despite the hardships, St. Nektarios never wavered in his devotion to Christ and his call to serve the Church. His humility, patience, and love for the people of God became legendary.

One of the most famous stories about St. Nektarios occurred during his later years while he was living at a convent on the island of Aegina. A young woman who had been paralyzed for many years was brought to the convent, hoping for a miracle. After hearing of the bishop's holiness, her family believed that through his prayers, she might be healed. St. Nektarios, deeply moved by the woman's faith, led her into the chapel, anointed her with oil, and fervently prayed for her healing. As the prayers concluded, the woman stood up, completely healed, and began to walk.

St. Nektarios, a humble servant of God, knew that the healing power did not come from him but from the grace of the Holy Spirit working through his **ordination**. As a bishop, he bore the responsibility of ministering to the people, administering the sacraments, and leading others to Christ. The miraculous healing was a testament not only to the holiness of St. Nektarios but also to the power of **Holy Orders**, through which God continues to work in His Church.

This story about St. Nektarios illustrates the sacred and profound role of **Holy Orders** in the Church. Through this sacrament, bishops, priests, and deacons are called to serve Christ and His people, not through their own strength, but through the grace imparted to them at their ordination. It is through this grace that the clergy are able to lead, teach, and administer the sacraments, ensuring the continuity of the apostolic ministry established by Christ Himself.

The Role of Holy Orders in the Life of the Church

In Orthodox Christianity, the **sacrament of Holy Orders** is the means by which the Church continues the ministry of the Apostles, perpetuating the apostolic succession through the ordained clergy. This sacrament is essential for the life of the Church, as it provides the Church with bishops, priests, and deacons who serve the people of God by administering the sacraments, preaching the Gospel, and guiding the faithful on the path to salvation.

Holy Orders is not merely a functional role or an ecclesiastical office; it is a **sacramental mystery**, a calling from God to participate in Christ's own priesthood. Through this sacrament, the ordained minister receives **grace** to serve the Church in a unique and sacred way, becoming a visible representative of Christ's presence in the world. The clergy are called to live lives of holiness, humility, and service, dedicating themselves to the spiritual care of the faithful and the continuation of the mission of the Church.

In this chapter, we will explore the nature of Holy Orders, its foundation in Scripture and Tradition, and its role in the life of the Church. We will also contrast the Orthodox understanding of Holy Orders with certain **Protestant** and **Roman Catholic** views, and examine the spiritual responsibilities that come with ordination.

The Apostolic Foundation of Holy Orders

The sacrament of Holy Orders has its foundation in the ministry of **Christ and the Apostles**. Jesus, during His earthly ministry, chose the Twelve Apostles and gave them the authority to preach, teach, and administer the sacraments in His name. After His resurrection, Jesus further empowered the Apostles by giving them the **Holy Spirit** and the authority to forgive sins (John 20:22-23), and to continue His work of proclaiming the Kingdom of God.

This apostolic authority was passed on through the laying on of hands, a practice known as **apostolic succession**. In **Acts 6:1-6**, the Apostles lay their hands on seven men who are chosen to serve as the first deacons, showing that from the earliest days of the Church, ordination was seen as the means by which spiritual authority was conferred. This practice continues in the Orthodox Church today, as bishops, priests, and deacons are ordained through the laying on of hands by a bishop, who himself stands in the line of apostolic succession.

The importance of apostolic succession cannot be overstated, as it ensures that the Church remains connected to the ministry of Christ and the Apostles. The bishops, as successors of the Apostles, are the guardians of the **faith**, the **sacraments**, and the unity of the Church. Through the sacrament of Holy Orders, the Church continues to be led by those who have received the grace and authority to teach, sanctify, and govern in Christ's name.

The Three Degrees of Holy Orders

In Orthodox Christianity, there are **three degrees** of Holy Orders: **bishop**, **priest**, and **deacon**. Each of these orders serves a unique and essential role in the life of the Church.

1. **Bishop**

    The **bishop** is the highest order of clergy and is considered a successor to the Apostles. Bishops are entrusted with the responsibility of overseeing the Church in a particular region, known as a **diocese**. They are the chief shepherds of their flock, responsible for teaching the faith, administering the sacraments, and maintaining the unity of the Church. Only bishops have the authority to ordain other clergy, including priests and deacons, and they play a crucial role in preserving the apostolic succession.

The bishop is seen as a visible representative of **Christ the High Priest** and is responsible for ensuring that the sacraments are administered properly and that the faith is faithfully transmitted to future generations. The bishop is also a guardian of Church unity, working to preserve the bond of love and faith among the various parishes and dioceses within the wider Orthodox communion.

124

2. **Priest**

   The **priest**, also called a **presbyter**, serves under the authority of the bishop and is responsible for the pastoral care of a particular community, often a parish. The priest's primary role is to administer the sacraments—especially the **Eucharist, Baptism, Chrismation, Confession, Marriage**, and **Holy Unction**—and to teach the faith. Priests are called to preach the Gospel, guide their parishioners in spiritual growth, and act as **spiritual fathers** to their communities.

Priests are seen as **icons of Christ**, serving as a visible representation of His presence in the world. While the priest does not have the fullness of apostolic authority (which belongs to the bishop), he shares in the bishop's ministry by administering the sacraments and shepherding the faithful. The priest acts as a bridge between the people and God, offering the people's prayers and sacrifices to God through the liturgical life of the Church.

3. **Deacon**

   The **deacon** is the first degree of ordained ministry and serves primarily as an assistant to the bishop and priest. The deacon's role is one of **service**, both in the liturgical life of the Church and in the

125

practical ministry to the needs of the community. In the Divine Liturgy, the deacon leads prayers, assists the priest at the altar, and has a role in proclaiming the Gospel. Deacons also serve the community by helping with charitable works, visiting the sick, and caring for the poor.

The role of the deacon is deeply rooted in the example of **Christ the Servant**, who came "not to be served, but to serve" (Mark 10:45). Deacons are called to embody this spirit of service, reminding the faithful that the heart of Christian ministry is humility and love.

The Grace of Holy Orders

Like all sacraments, Holy Orders is a means by which God imparts His **grace** to the individual who is ordained. This grace is not only for the benefit of the ordained person but for the benefit of the entire Church. The grace of Holy Orders enables bishops, priests, and deacons to carry out their ministry with the strength and wisdom of the Holy Spirit, serving the people of God with humility and love.

The grace given in Holy Orders allows the ordained minister to act as a **living icon of Christ**. Through this grace, the clergy are empowered to administer the sacraments, preach the Gospel, and guide the faithful in

126

their spiritual lives. This grace is not something the clergy can achieve on their own; it is a divine gift that enables them to fulfill their sacred responsibilities.

St. John Chrysostom speaks of the high calling of the priesthood, reminding us that "the priesthood is performed on earth, but it ranks among heavenly ordinances." The grace of Holy Orders transforms the natural abilities of the clergy, making them instruments of God's work in the world.

Contrasting Protestant and Roman Catholic Views of Holy Orders

The Orthodox understanding of Holy Orders contrasts with both **Protestant** and **Roman Catholic** views. In many **Protestant** traditions, the idea of a sacramental priesthood is rejected in favor of the concept of the **priesthood of all believers**. While Protestant ministers may still be ordained, the ordination is often viewed as a **functional role** rather than a sacramental mystery that imparts divine grace. As a result, the sacramental nature of ministry and the continuity of apostolic succession are often lost in Protestant theology.

In contrast, the **Roman Catholic** Church shares with Orthodoxy the belief in the sacramental nature of Holy Orders and the importance of apostolic succession.

However, there are key differences in the understanding of the **role of the priesthood**. In Roman Catholic theology, the priest is often understood to act **in persona Christi**, meaning "in the person of Christ," particularly in the administration of the sacraments. This concept emphasizes the priest's unique role in standing in for Christ in the liturgy and the sacraments.

In Orthodoxy, while the priest is certainly a representative of Christ, the emphasis is on the priest as a **living icon of Christ**, rather than acting in Christ's person. The priest, deacon, or bishop points the faithful to Christ, always reminding them that it is Christ who is the true **High Priest**, and it is through His grace that the sacraments are made effective. The priest is not seen as replacing Christ but as making Christ present in a sacramental way through his ministry

Spiritual Responsibilities of the Ordained Clergy

Those who receive Holy Orders take on significant **spiritual responsibilities**. The clergy are called to a life of **holiness**, **humility**, and **self-sacrifice**, serving as shepherds of the flock and spiritual guides to the faithful. They are responsible for administering the sacraments, teaching the faith, and providing pastoral care to their communities. In addition to their liturgical duties, clergy are often involved in counseling, visiting the sick, comforting the grieving, and helping parishioners grow in their spiritual lives.

Ordained clergy are also responsible for guarding the **faith** and **tradition** of the Church, ensuring that the teachings of the Apostles are faithfully preserved and passed on to future generations. The role of the clergy is not one of power or authority for its own sake, but of **service**—to God and to His people. The clergy are called to follow Christ's example, who said, "I am among you as one who serves" (Luke 22:27).

Chapter 8. Concluding Prayer

O Lord Jesus Christ, our High Priest and Good Shepherd, who called the Apostles to follow You and to serve Your Church, bless all those who are called to the sacrament of Holy Orders. Strengthen them with Your grace, guide them in their ministry, and help them to lead Your people with love, humility, and faithfulness. May they always serve as living icons of Your presence in the world, pointing the way to Your kingdom. For You are holy, now and ever and unto ages of ages. Amen.

Chapter 8. Review Questions

What is the primary purpose of the sacrament of Holy Orders?

- o A) To provide leadership in the Church
- o B) To continue the apostolic ministry of the Church and to impart grace for administering the sacraments and teaching the faith
- o C) To give clergy authority over laypeople
- o D) To allow for a hierarchical structure in the Church

What is the significance of apostolic succession in Orthodox Christianity?

- o A) It ensures that the clergy have the proper education
- o B) It connects the clergy to the original Apostles and preserves the authority and unity of the Church
- o C) It gives the clergy the power to control the Church
- o D) It guarantees the financial stability of the Church

What are the three degrees of Holy Orders in Orthodox Christianity?

- o A) Bishop, Priest, and Deacon
- o B) Pastor, Minister, and Teacher
- o C) Pope, Cardinal, and Priest
- o D) Layperson, Monk, and Priest

How does Orthodox theology view the priest's role during the sacraments?

- o A) The priest acts as a representative of the people
- o B) The priest acts in persona Christi (in the person of Christ)
- o C) The priest serves as a living icon of Christ, pointing the people to Him
- o D) The priest acts independently of the Church

What is the primary role of the deacon in Orthodox Christianity?

- o A) To replace the priest when necessary
- o B) To assist the bishop and priest in both liturgical and practical service
- o C) To teach the faith in place of the bishop

- o D) To administer all sacraments except for ordination

These review questions encourage deeper reflection on the nature of Holy Orders, the role of clergy in the life of the Church, and the theological distinctions that make the Orthodox view of ordination unique.

Chapter 9

The Sacrament of Holy Unction
Healing for Body and Soul

The Sacrament of Healing in Orthodox Christianity

The life of St. John of Kronstadt, a beloved Russian
saint of the 19th century, is filled with stories of miraculous
healing through prayer and the sacraments. One day, a
desperate mother came to him with her dying child, who
was suffering from a severe illness. Doctors had given up
hope, and the family had been preparing for the worst. With
tears in her eyes, the mother begged St. John to pray for her
child's healing.

Moved with compassion, St. John took a small bottle of
holy oil, blessed in the sacrament of Holy Unction, and
gently anointed the child, praying for God's healing grace
to descend upon the little one. He asked for the intercession
of the Theotokos and all the saints, entrusting the child's
life to God's mercy. That night, the child's fever broke, and
within a few days, he was completely healed. The mother
returned to St. John, overwhelmed with gratitude, thanking
God for the miraculous healing that had taken place.

This powerful story of healing through Holy Unction
illustrates the profound mystery of this sacrament, where
God's grace works through the anointing with holy oil to
bring healing not only to the body but also to the soul.
Through the prayers of the Church, God's healing power is

made manifest in the lives of the faithful, offering hope and restoration in times of suffering.

This story provides an example of how Holy Unction functions in the life of the Church, where the faithful, through prayer and anointing, can experience both physical and spiritual healing. St. John of Kronstadt's deep faith and reliance on God's mercy through the sacraments is a model for all who seek healing and comfort in times of illness.

The Sacrament of Healing in Orthodox Christianity

One of the most remarkable stories of healing in the Orthodox tradition comes from the life of **St. Nektarios of Aegina**, a modern-day saint known for his great compassion and healing miracles. St. Nektarios was a bishop in Greece, and throughout his life, many people sought his prayers for physical and spiritual healing. After his repose in 1920, his intercessions continued to work miracles, particularly for those suffering from cancer and other serious illnesses.

One such story involves a woman who had been diagnosed with terminal cancer. After medical treatments failed, she traveled to Aegina to seek the prayers of St. Nektarios. She was anointed with **holy oil** at his monastery, and shortly after, the cancerous tumors disappeared. The doctors were astounded, unable to explain her sudden recovery. This miraculous healing is one of many attributed to the intercessions of St. Nektarios, and it illustrates the profound power of **Holy Unction** and the role of the saints in the Church's ministry of healing.

Holy Unction, as a sacrament, embodies this mystery of divine healing. Through the grace of God and the prayers of the Church, Holy Unction brings both **physical** and **spiritual** restoration, reminding us that healing encompasses the whole person—body, soul, and spirit.

Healing the Whole Person: The Purpose of Holy Unction

In Orthodox Christianity, human beings are viewed as a unity of **body and soul**. This means that physical illness cannot be isolated from the spiritual condition of a person. Just as we seek healing for physical ailments, we must also seek healing for the wounds of sin and the brokenness of our souls. The sacrament of Holy Unction addresses both of these dimensions, bringing healing to body and soul alike.

The primary purpose of Holy Unction is **healing** in a broad sense. While physical healing may occur, the sacrament also brings **spiritual strength**, **peace**, and the **forgiveness of sins**. In this way, it mirrors the holistic view of salvation in Orthodoxy: God's saving grace touches every part of our being, not just our souls but our bodies as well. Even when physical healing does not occur, Holy Unction strengthens the person's relationship with God and prepares them to face suffering, and even death, with faith and hope.

For Orthodox Christians, the purpose of Holy Unction is not only to ask for physical recovery but to invite God's presence into our suffering. Healing can manifest as peace, patience, or endurance in the face of illness. It is a reminder that our hope is not merely in this life but in the **resurrection** to come.

The Scriptural Foundation of Holy Unction

The sacrament of Holy Unction has its foundation in **Scripture**, particularly in the Epistle of **James 5:14-15**:

"Is anyone among you sick? Let him call for the elders of the church, and let them pray over him, anointing him with oil in the name of the Lord. And the prayer of faith will save the one who is sick, and the Lord will raise him up. And if he has committed sins, he will be forgiven."

This passage encapsulates the dual purpose of Holy Unction: **healing** and **forgiveness of sins**. The anointing with oil is not merely symbolic but sacramental. The oil, blessed through the prayers of the Church, becomes a means of **grace**, offering both physical relief and spiritual restoration.

The ministry of healing is also evident in the life of Christ and His Apostles. In **Mark 6:13**, we read that the Apostles "anointed with oil many who were sick and healed them." Jesus Himself often healed the sick, and He sent His Apostles out to continue this ministry, demonstrating that healing is an essential part of the Church's mission. Through Holy Unction, the Church continues Christ's healing work, offering the faithful an opportunity to encounter God's grace in their moments of suffering.

Holy Unction as a Sacrament of the Church

Holy Unction is one of the seven sacraments of the Orthodox Church, and it is administered by a **priest** or **bishop** through the anointing of the sick person with **holy oil**. The sacrament is not reserved only for those on their deathbed, as some might think, but it can be administered to anyone in need of God's healing grace. It is often offered to those suffering from chronic illness, emotional distress, or even spiritual weariness.

The sacrament is most frequently performed in private, though it is also administered to the whole congregation on

Holy Wednesday during **Holy Week**. This communal celebration of Holy Unction reminds the faithful that we are all in need of healing, whether it is physical or spiritual. In this sense, Holy Unction is a sacrament of renewal and restoration for the entire body of Christ, the Church.

During the service, there are **seven readings** from the Gospels, **seven prayers**, and **seven anointings**, representing the **sevenfold grace** of the Holy Spirit. The prayers focus on healing, forgiveness, and restoration, asking God to deliver the sick from their afflictions and grant them peace. The oil, consecrated during the service, is the visible sign of God's healing power at work.

Healing and the Forgiveness of Sins

A key aspect of Holy Unction is its connection to the **forgiveness of sins**. As **James 5** makes clear, the anointing with oil and the prayers of the Church bring not only physical healing but also the grace of **spiritual restoration**. This reflects the Orthodox understanding that physical illness and spiritual suffering are often intertwined. Even though personal sin is not always the cause of illness, the effects of sin—both individual and communal—can have a profound impact on our physical and emotional health.

Holy Unction offers healing for the whole person, addressing both the body's needs and the soul's need for reconciliation with God. This sacrament reminds us that ultimate healing comes from God, and that the forgiveness of sins is essential for our spiritual well-being. The sacrament brings peace to the soul, freeing it from the burden of sin and allowing the person to experience God's mercy in a profound way.

Holy Unction is also part of the Church's ministry to those approaching the end of their lives. In these cases, the sacrament prepares the person for **eternal life**, offering them forgiveness, peace, and strength as they transition from this life to the next. The sacrament helps the person face death with **hope in the resurrection**, reminding them that death is not the end but the beginning of new life in Christ.

Contrasting Protestant Views of Healing

In some **Protestant** traditions, healing is often viewed in terms of **miraculous cures**, with healing services focusing on dramatic recoveries from illness as a sign of God's favor. While Orthodox Christianity certainly believes in the power of God to perform miracles, the emphasis in Holy Unction is on **holistic healing**—the healing of the whole person, body, soul, and spirit. Physical healing may or may not occur, but the sacrament always brings the **peace of Christ** and the **forgiveness of sins**.

For Orthodox Christians, healing is not always immediate or miraculous. Sometimes healing comes in the form of **spiritual strength** to endure suffering, or in the deep **peace** that allows a person to accept God's will, even if that means carrying the cross of illness. Holy Unction is not about guaranteeing a cure but about bringing the person into **closer communion** with God, allowing His grace to work in whatever way is needed for their salvation.

This approach contrasts with certain Protestant views that may prioritize physical healing as the primary evidence of faith. In Orthodoxy, the focus is on the **sacramental encounter** with God's grace, which heals and restores the entire person, regardless of the physical outcome.

Holy Unction and Preparation for Eternal Life

Holy Unction is not only a sacrament of healing for those who are sick; it is also a sacrament of **preparation for eternal life**. When administered to those near death, the sacrament offers **spiritual strength** and **peace** as the person prepares to meet the Lord. This aspect of Holy Unction, sometimes referred to as the "anointing of the dying," is not about curing the body but about preparing the soul for its journey into the Kingdom of God.

The prayers of Holy Unction ask for both physical healing and the **grace to endure suffering** with faith. For those who are nearing the end of life, the sacrament provides the strength to face death with **hope**, knowing that through Christ's resurrection, death has been overcome. Holy Unction assures the faithful that they are not alone in their suffering, for Christ is with them, offering His peace and preparing them for eternal life.

The Importance of Holy Unction in Christian Life

While Holy Unction is most often associated with physical illness, it is a sacrament that can be received at various times in life, whenever the faithful are in need of God's healing grace. Just as we regularly receive the sacraments of Confession and the Eucharist for our spiritual health, so too can we receive Holy Unction to heal the wounds of body and soul. It is a sacrament of **renewal**, offering God's mercy and grace to those who are suffering in any way.

Through Holy Unction, we encounter the **compassion of God**, who desires our complete healing. Whether we are suffering from physical pain, emotional turmoil, or spiritual dryness, this sacrament offers us the grace to be restored and renewed. It is a powerful reminder that God is always with us, even in our suffering, and that His grace is sufficient to carry us through every trial.

Chapter 9. Concluding Prayer

O Lord Jesus Christ, the Physician of our souls and bodies, who healed the sick and gave sight to the blind, grant Your healing grace to all who come to You in faith. Heal us of our infirmities, both physical and spiritual, and forgive us our sins. Strengthen us in our suffering, and grant us peace and hope in Your resurrection. For You are the source of all healing, and to You we give glory, together with the Father and the Holy Spirit, now and ever and unto ages of ages. Amen.

Chapter 9 Review Questions

What is the primary purpose of the sacrament of Holy Unction in Orthodox Christianity?

- o A) To guarantee physical healing
- o B) To provide spiritual healing and the forgiveness of sins, and possibly physical healing
- o C) To anoint the dying

- D) To offer an alternative to medical care

What is the significance of the anointing with oil in Holy Unction?

- A) It is a symbolic act without real effect
- B) It represents the healing grace of God, bringing both physical and spiritual restoration
- C) It is only for those who are dying
- D) It is primarily a social or cultural practice

Which passage from the New Testament provides the biblical foundation for Holy Unction?

- A) Matthew 28:19
- B) James 5:14-15
- C) John 3:16
- D) Luke 22:19

How does Orthodox Christianity view healing through Holy Unction?

- A) It focuses exclusively on miraculous physical cures
- B) It emphasizes holistic healing—physical, spiritual, and emotional

- C) It discourages seeking medical care
- D) It guarantees a quick recovery from illness

How does Holy Unction prepare someone for eternal life?

- A) By removing all illness from the body
- B) By offering forgiveness, peace, and spiritual strength to face death with hope
- C) By guaranteeing a longer life
- D) By preventing future suffering

These review questions aim to deepen the reader's understanding of Holy Unction as a sacrament of healing, grace, and spiritual renewal in Orthodox Christianity.

Chapter 10

The Church—The Body of Christ and the Community of Salvation

The Church as the Mystical Body of Christ

A Story from the Life of St. Ignatius of Antioch: A Witness to Apostolic Authority and Unity

The life of **St. Ignatius of Antioch** (35–107 AD) offers a powerful testimony to the Church's unity and authority, rooted in **Apostolic Succession**. As a disciple of the Apostle John and bishop of Antioch, Ignatius taught that the Church is not a human organization but the **living Body of Christ**, where believers are united through the **sacraments** and **apostolic governance**.

On his way to Rome to face martyrdom, Ignatius wrote letters urging Christians to remain in communion with their **bishops**, saying:

"Wherever the bishop appears, there let the people be; even as, wherever Jesus Christ is, there is the Catholic Church" (Letter to the Smyrnaeans, 8).

Ignatius understood the bishop's role as a **visible sign of unity** in the Church. **Unity with the bishop meant unity with Christ**, because the bishop's authority came through an unbroken line of **Apostolic Succession**, passed down from the Apostles. For Ignatius, salvation was found only within the Church, the Mystical Body of Christ.

The Church as the Mystical Body of Christ

The Orthodox Church teaches that the Church is the **Mystical Body of Christ** (1 Corinthians 12:27), where believers are united with Christ and one another through the **sacraments and the power of the Holy Spirit**. This unity is both **visible and spiritual**. Through the sacraments—such as **Baptism, Chrismation, and the Eucharist**—believers receive the grace that transforms them into **living members of Christ's Body**.

The Four Marks of the Church: One, Holy, Catholic, and Apostolic

The **Nicene Creed** defines the Church with four essential marks: **One, Holy, Catholic, and Apostolic**. These marks ensure the Church remains faithful to the teachings of Christ and distinguishes the **authentic Church** from other communities that have **departed from the Apostolic Faith**.

1. One

The Church is **one** because it is united in **Christ, the Head of the Body** (Ephesians 4:4-6). This unity is preserved through the **common faith, sacraments, and leadership of bishops** in Apostolic Succession.

2. Holy

The Church is **holy** because it is sanctified by **Christ's presence** and offers believers the means to grow in holiness through the **sacraments**.

3. Catholic

The Church is **catholic** because it offers the **fullness of the faith** to all people, at all times and places.

4. Apostolic

The Church is **apostolic** because it continues the mission of the Apostles through **Apostolic Succession**, ensuring the sacraments and teachings remain valid and unchanged.

Sacramental Validity in Orthodoxy

In Orthodoxy, **sacramental validity** is tied to **Apostolic Succession**. Only priests and bishops ordained within this unbroken succession can administer valid sacraments. Sacraments outside Apostolic Succession may be sincere acts of faith, but they **lack the full grace** conferred by Christ through His Church.

The Three-Legged Stool: Scripture, Tradition, and Apostolic Succession

The Orthodox Church rests on a **three-legged stool,** with **Scripture, Tradition, and Apostolic Succession** as its foundation.

- **Scripture**: The Bible is essential but is interpreted **within the life of the Church.**
- **Tradition**: Tradition preserves the teachings and practices of the Apostles through councils, liturgy, and writings.
- **Apostolic Succession**: Apostolic Succession guarantees the authority of the sacraments and ensures the continuity of the faith.

Communities that reject one or more legs—such as **sola scriptura** Protestantism or Roman Catholic reliance on **papal infallibility**—lose the stability provided by the Church.

Chapter 10. Concluding Prayer

O Lord Jesus Christ, Head of the Church, we thank You for the gift of Your Body, through which we are united to You and one another. Strengthen us to remain faithful to the unity, holiness, catholicity, and apostolic nature of Your Church. May we grow in Your grace through the sacraments and walk the narrow path that leads to life. Through the prayers of St. Ignatius of Antioch and all the saints, now and ever, and unto ages of ages. Amen.

Chapter 10. Chapter Review Questions

What ensures the validity of the sacraments in the Orthodox Church?

- o A) Personal faith of the priest
- o B) Apostolic Succession
- o C) The use of correct liturgical words
- o D) The holiness of the congregation

What role do bishops play in the Orthodox Church?

- o A) Independent rulers of local communities
- o B) Living icons of Christ who teach, sanctify, and guide the faithful
- o C) Sole interpreters of Scripture

  D) Figureheads without real authority

How does the Orthodox Church differ from Roman Catholicism in governance?

- o A) Both rely on the authority of the pope
- o B) Both rely on individual councils alone

o   C) Orthodoxy uses a conciliar model, while Catholicism emphasizes papal infallibility

D) Orthodoxy has no bishops

What are the three legs of the metaphorical stool representing the Orthodox Church?

o   A) Faith, Hope, and Love

o   B) Scripture, Tradition, and Apostolic Succession

o   C) Liturgy, Doctrine, and Devotion

D) Fasting, Prayer, and Almsgiving

Why is Apostolic Succession essential in the Orthodox Church?

o   A) It is only a symbolic tradition

o   B) It ensures the validity of the sacraments and preserves the Apostolic Faith

o   C) It allows for continuous innovation in doctrine

o   D) It is a requirement for priestly ordination but has no other significance

Chapter 11

The Holy Eucharist—The Source and Summit of the Christian Life

The Eucharist and Its Role in Orthodox Christian Life and Theosis

A Story from the Life of St. Seraphim of Sarov: The Radiance of Eucharistic Life

St. Seraphim of Sarov (1754–1833) lived a life of deep asceticism, prayer, and fasting, all centered on his participation in the **Eucharist**. Known for his profound inner peace and spiritual radiance, St. Seraphim often taught that **the Eucharist is the true source of spiritual life**, sustaining believers in their journey toward **theosis—** union with God.

On one occasion, a visitor witnessed St. Seraphim's face shining with an unearthly light as he spoke about the work of the Holy Spirit in those who partake of the Eucharist with faith. He explained that the grace of the Eucharist transforms the soul, enabling believers to grow in **the likeness of God**. St. Seraphim's life demonstrates that **the Eucharist, supported by fasting, prayer, and ascetic discipline, leads to theosis—**the process of becoming partakers of the divine nature.

Theosis: The Goal of the Christian Life

In Orthodox Christianity, **theosis** is the goal of the spiritual life. It is not merely about moral improvement or religious observance—it is about **participating in the divine life** and being transformed into the likeness of Christ. The Eucharist plays a central role in this process, for in the Eucharist, believers **receive the real Body and Blood of Christ**, which nourishes the soul and imparts divine grace.

Theosis is not achieved by human effort alone but through **synergy**—the cooperation between human effort and God's grace. **Prayer, fasting, Confession, and the Eucharist** work together to transform the believer, leading them from sin and brokenness to **union with God**. As St. Athanasius famously said:

"God became man so that man might become god."

This transformation is made possible through the sacraments, especially the Eucharist, where believers **participate directly in the life of Christ**.

The Role of Asceticism in Supporting the Eucharist

Asceticism—the practice of fasting, prayer, self-discipline, and self-denial—supports the Eucharistic life by helping believers prepare their hearts to receive Christ worthily. Fasting, in particular, teaches believers to **discipline their desires** and develop reliance on God rather than material things.

In Orthodox tradition, fasting is not just about abstaining from certain foods but about cultivating a **humble and repentant heart**. Asceticism creates the spiritual space needed for **the grace of the Eucharist to take root** in the soul. As St. John Chrysostom taught:

"Fasting is the support of our soul: it gives us wings to ascend on high and to obtain the true heights. But without the Eucharist, fasting alone is insufficient to bring us into union with God."

Asceticism without the Eucharist is incomplete. It is only through the **Body and Blood of Christ** that believers receive the divine life needed for **theosis**.

Can Fasting Replace the Eucharist?

While fasting plays a crucial role in the spiritual life, **it cannot replace the Eucharist**. Jesus' words in **John 6:53** emphasize the centrality of the Eucharist:

"Unless you eat the flesh of the Son of Man and drink His blood, you have no life in you."

156

Fasting prepares the heart to receive the Eucharist, but the sacrament itself is the **source of divine life**. Without the Eucharist, fasting becomes a mere exercise in self-denial, lacking the grace that comes from direct **communion with Christ**. Just as a field must be watered to produce fruit, the soul must be nourished by the Eucharist to grow in **the likeness of God**.

Icons and Theosis: Windows into Heaven

Icons hold a significant place in the Orthodox spiritual life, playing an essential role in **theosis**. Icons are not merely religious art; they are **"windows into heaven"**, providing a visual encounter with the divine. Through icons, believers are reminded that they are surrounded by a "great cloud of witnesses" (Hebrews 12:1) and are called to **participate in the divine life** alongside the saints.

When Orthodox Christians venerate icons, they are not worshiping the material image but honoring the **reality that the icon represents**—Christ, the Theotokos (Mother of God), or the saints. The **veneration of icons** fosters intimacy with Christ and His saints, inspiring believers to **follow their example and grow in holiness**. Icons also **teach theology visually**, depicting key events from

Scripture and the lives of the saints, reminding believers of the truths of the faith.

By gazing upon and praying with icons, believers develop a deeper sense of **God's presence** in their lives, drawing them closer to **theosis**.

The Rejection of Icons by Other Christian Traditions

Many **Protestant communities** reject the use of icons, believing that **visual representations of Christ and the saints** violate the commandment against graven images (Exodus 20:4). This rejection stems from the **iconoclastic controversies** of the early Church, when some argued that the use of images in worship was idolatrous. However, the **Seventh Ecumenical Council (787)** affirmed the use of icons, declaring that since **God became visible in the Incarnation of Christ**, it is appropriate to depict Him in visual form.

Orthodoxy teaches that icons are not idols but **sacramental means of encountering God**. Just as the Eucharist is the real presence of Christ under the forms of bread and wine, **icons are a visible way of experiencing the divine presence**. The rejection of icons by some Christian traditions reflects a **reduced sacramental**

understanding, focusing on the internal and abstract aspects of faith while missing the **incarnational reality** of God's presence in the material world.

Seasonal Fasting and the Eucharistic Life

Orthodox fasting follows a **liturgical rhythm** that aligns the lives of believers with the life of Christ and the saints. The four major fasting seasons prepare the faithful for significant **feasts and Eucharistic celebrations**, fostering repentance, renewal, and deeper communion with God.

The Four Major Fasting Seasons:

1. **Great Lent**
   - A time of repentance and preparation for **Pascha (Easter)**, focusing on prayer, fasting, and Confession. The Eucharist during Pascha becomes the **culmination of the Lenten journey**.

2. **The Nativity Fast**
   - Leading up to **Christmas**, this fast prepares believers to celebrate the Incarnation of Christ. It emphasizes **charity, prayer, and Eucharistic participation**.

3. **The Apostles' Fast**

- A time of reflection on the missionary work of the Church, culminating in the feast of **Saints Peter and Paul**. This fast encourages believers to grow in **spiritual discipline and Eucharistic devotion**.

4. **The Dormition Fast**
   - This fast honors the **falling asleep of the Theotokos** and encourages believers to imitate her humility and faith. It concludes with a celebration of the Eucharist in honor of Mary, the Mother of God.

Hospitality, Catechesis, and Closed Communion in HOCACOA

The **Holy Orthodox Catholic and Apostolic Church of America (HOCACOA)** practices **closed communion**, reserving the Eucharist for baptized Orthodox Christians who have prepared through fasting, prayer, and Confession. However, newcomers are always **welcome to attend the Divine Liturgy**. After the service, they are often **invited to join catechism classes** to learn more about the Orthodox faith and prepare for full participation in the sacraments.

The practice of closed communion is rooted in the belief that the **Eucharist is a declaration of unity in faith**

and doctrine. To receive the Eucharist without sharing in the full faith of the Church would create a **contradiction**. Yet, the Church's approach is always one of **hospitality and love**, seeking to guide newcomers into a deeper understanding of the **Eucharist and the life of faith**.

The Eucharist: A Foretaste of the Kingdom of God

The Eucharist offers believers a **foretaste of the heavenly banquet**, uniting them with the saints and angels in eternal worship. Each Divine Liturgy anticipates the final fulfillment of God's Kingdom, where Christ will reign in glory.

As St. Paul writes:

"For as often as you eat this bread and drink the cup, you proclaim the Lord's death until He comes" (1 Corinthians 11:26).

Through the Eucharist, believers are strengthened to **walk the narrow path of salvation**, receiving the grace needed to grow in **faith, hope, and love**.

Chapter 11. Concluding Prayer

O Lord Jesus Christ, who gives us Your Body and Blood as the bread of life and the cup of salvation, help us to receive this sacrament with faith, love, and reverence. Through prayer, fasting, and the veneration of icons, lead us on the path of theosis, that we may grow in Your likeness and participate in Your divine life. Unite us with You and with one another, and bring us into the joy of Your eternal Kingdom. Through the prayers of St. Seraphim of Sarov and all the saints, now and ever, and unto ages of ages. Amen.

Chapter 11. Chapter Review Questions

What is the goal of theosis?

- o A) To follow religious rules.
- o B) To become united with God through divine grace.
- o C) To achieve personal success.
- o D) To earn salvation through good deeds.

What is the purpose of fasting in Orthodox Christianity?

- A) To punish the body.
- B) To prepare the soul for receiving the Eucharist and deepen one's relationship with God.
- C) To follow cultural traditions.
- D) To improve physical health.

2. **How do icons aid in theosis?**

- A) They replace the need for prayer.
- B) They provide a visual encounter with the divine and inspire spiritual **growth.**
- C) They are used only for decoration.
- D) They offer historical information about saints.

3. **Why does the Orthodox Church practice closed communion?**

- A) To exclude outsiders.
- B) To preserve unity in faith and sacramental life.
- C) To enforce rules.
- D) To limit participation.

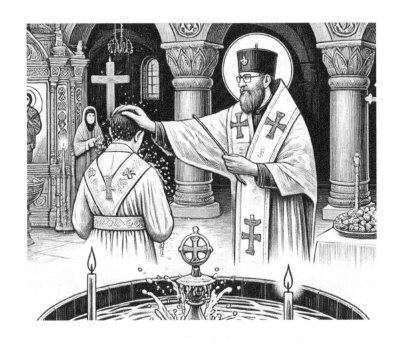

Chapter 12

Baptism and Chrismation
The Sacraments of Initiation
into the Christian Life

The Role of Baptism, Chrismation, Repentance, and Salvation in Orthodox Christianity

A Story from the Life of St. Vladimir the Great: A Nation Baptized into Christ

St. **Vladimir the Great** (c. 958–1015) offers a profound example of the transformative power of **baptism and repentance**. Once a violent pagan ruler, Vladimir sought truth beyond the empty promises of his ancestors' gods. Inspired by the reports of his emissaries, who had witnessed the beauty of the **Divine Liturgy** in Constantinople, Vladimir embraced Orthodox Christianity. His baptism in 988 not only transformed his personal character—leading him to rule with justice and mercy—but also marked the beginning of a new era for his entire nation, as the people of **Kievan Rus** followed him into the Christian faith.

Despite his baptism, Vladimir's life was not without struggle. Like all believers, he had to continually **repent** for his shortcomings and rely on the **grace of the sacraments** to stay on the narrow path to salvation. His story teaches us that baptism is only the beginning of the Christian journey—a journey that requires **ongoing** repentance, cooperation with God's grace (synergy), and growth toward theosis (union with God).

Orthodoxy and Religious Pluralism: A Compassionate Response

Orthodoxy affirms that **Christ is the only way to salvation** (John 14:6), but it also acknowledges that **God's mercy extends beyond the visible boundaries of the Church**. The Church does not claim to know how God will judge those of other faiths but trusts that His **justice is perfectly balanced with His mercy**.

St. Paul teaches:

"God desires all people to be saved and to come to the knowledge of the truth" (1 Timothy 2:4).

The Orthodox Church holds that while **the fullness of salvation is found within the Church**—through participation in the sacraments, prayer, and repentance—God may also work **in mysterious ways** in the lives of those outside the Church. **Seeds of truth** may be present in other religions, but these truths find their **ultimate fulfillment** in Christ and the life of the Church.

Orthodoxy maintains that **religious pluralism**—the idea that all religions are equally valid paths to God—is incompatible with the teachings of Christ. However, the

Church approaches individuals of other faiths with **humility, compassion, and a spirit of dialogue**, recognizing that all people are made in the image of God and called to know Him.

Baptism and the Role of Repentance Post-Baptism

Baptism cleanses the believer from all sin and grants **spiritual rebirth,** marking the beginning of the Christian life. However, baptism does not mark the **end of the need for repentance**. The journey toward **theosis**—union with God—requires continuous **cooperation with God's grace (synergy)** and a lifelong commitment to repentance. As St. John the Theologian writes:

"If we say we have no sin, we deceive ourselves, and the truth is not in us. If we confess our sins, He is faithful and just to forgive us our sins and to cleanse us from all unrighteousness" (1 John 1:8-9).

The Role of Repentance in Synergy and Theosis

Synergy refers to the cooperation between **God's grace** and **human effort** in the process of salvation. While **baptism provides the initial grace** that sets the believer on the path to salvation, ongoing repentance ensures that the believer stays aligned with God's will. Every time a believer repents and returns to God, they grow closer to **theosis**—the process of becoming more like God.

Repentance, therefore, is not merely about **remorse for past sins** but about **reorienting the heart toward God** and participating more deeply in His divine life. Through repentance and the sacraments—particularly **Confession and the Eucharist**—believers are continually transformed by God's grace.

Orthodoxy's Response to "Once Saved, Always Saved"

Many Protestant traditions, particularly those influenced by **Reformed theology**, teach the concept of **"Once Saved, Always Saved."** This doctrine holds that once an individual makes a profession of faith in Christ, their salvation is eternally secure, regardless of their subsequent actions.

In contrast, **Orthodoxy rejects the idea that salvation as a one-time event.** Salvation is understood as a **lifelong process** that involves **faith, repentance, and participation in the sacraments.** While the grace received in baptism marks the beginning of this journey, believers are called to **persevere in faith and good works**, relying on God's grace at every step.

Orthodoxy teaches that salvation can be lost through **persistent unrepented sin** and rejection of God's grace. As St. Paul writes:

"Work out your own salvation with fear and trembling; for it is God who works in you, both to will and to work for His good pleasure" (Philippians 2:12-13).

This passage highlights the **synergistic nature of salvation**—it is both **God's work and our cooperation** with His grace. Just as **falling away from grace is possible**, repentance provides a way to return to God and **renew the grace** first received in baptism.

Baptism, Chrismation, and the Lifelong Journey of Faith

The Orthodox understanding of salvation emphasizes that baptism and chrismation are the **beginning of a lifelong journey** toward theosis. Chrismation, which follows baptism, **seals the gift of the Holy Spirit** upon the believer, equipping them for **spiritual warfare** and participation in the **life of the Church**.

However, the grace given in baptism and chrismation must be **nurtured** through **repentance, prayer, fasting, and participation in the sacraments**. The believer is called to actively cooperate with God's grace, growing in faith and love each day.

The Role of Godparents: Spiritual Mentors on the Narrow Path

Godparents, or **sponsors**, play a crucial role in the spiritual formation of the baptized. They stand as **spiritual guardians and mentors**, responsible for helping the baptized grow in faith and walk the narrow path toward salvation.

Godparents take on the responsibility to:

- **Pray for their godchild regularly.**
- Model a life of **faith and repentance**.
- Encourage participation in the **sacramental life** of the Church.
- Support the godchild in moments of **doubt or struggle**, reminding them of their baptismal identity.

In Orthodoxy, the relationship between godparents and godchildren reflects the **communal nature of salvation**, reminding believers that they do not walk the narrow path alone.

The Narrow Path vs. Modernist Views of Salvation

In **Orthodoxy**, salvation involves **faith, repentance, and participation in the sacraments**. It is a **narrow path that requires discipline and perseverance**. Modernist views, such as those expressed by **Pope Francis**, suggest a **broader understanding of salvation** that includes; **the unrepentant, atheists, and followers of other religions**. While Orthodoxy acknowledges that **God's mercy is limitless**, it insists that **salvation cannot be separated from the life of faith, Reconciliation, and the sacraments.**

The Orthodox Church teaches that the path to salvation is **difficult** and requires **ongoing repentance and cooperation with God's grace**. Expanding the boundaries of salvation to include those who reject Christ risks **leading people away from the narrow path**. Orthodoxy encourages all people to **seek the fullness of truth in Christ** and enter into the life of the Church through **baptism and chrismation**.

Chapter 12. Concluding Prayer

O Lord Jesus Christ, who called us to walk the narrow path that leads to life, strengthen us by Your grace to persevere in faith, repentance, and love. Help us to cooperate with Your Spirit in all things, growing each day in the likeness of Your divine image. Bless our godparents and spiritual mentors, that they may guide us faithfully on the path of salvation. Have mercy on those outside the Church, and draw all people into the fullness of Your truth. Through the prayers of St. Vladimir and all the saints, now and ever, and unto ages of ages. Amen.

Chapter 12. Chapter Review Questions

What role does repentance play after baptism?

- o A) It is unnecessary after baptism.
- o B) It reorients the heart toward God and renews the grace received in baptism.
- o C) It only applies to mortal sins.
- o D) It is purely symbolic.

What is the Orthodox understanding of salvation?

- o A) A one-time event at conversion.
- o B) A lifelong process of cooperation with God's grace through faith, repentance, and sacraments.
- o C) Guaranteed at baptism.
- o D) Reserved for the perfect.

How does Orthodoxy view religious pluralism?

- o A) God's mercy may extend to those outside the Church, but the fullness of salvation is found in Christ and the sacraments.
- o B) All religions are equally valid paths to God.
- o C) Salvation is exclusive to Orthodox Christians.
- o D) God saves everyone regardless of faith.

What is the concept of synergy in Orthodox theology?

- o A) Salvation is entirely human effort.
- o B) Salvation requires cooperation between divine grace and human effort.
- o C) Salvation is only God's work.
- o D) Synergy replaces faith.

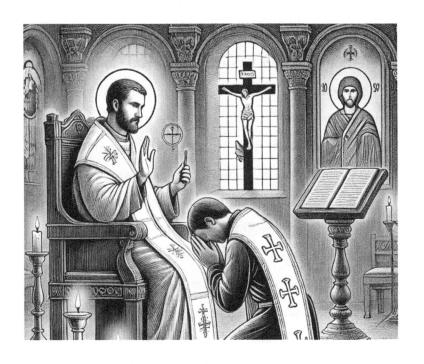

Chapter 13

**The Sacrament of
Confession
Healing, Spiritual Warfare,
and Fasting
The Sacrament of
Confession in Orthodox
Christianity**

A Story from the Life of St. Silouan the Athonite: Confession as a Step Toward Union with God

St. **Silouan the Athonite** began his spiritual journey with great zeal after joining a monastery on Mount Athos. Early in his monastic life, he experienced profound spiritual joy. However, this joy soon gave way to an intense struggle, as he battled **temptations and doubts** about his salvation. Silouan turned frequently to **Confession and repentance**, seeking guidance from his spiritual father. He confessed his weaknesses, frustrations, and struggles with pride, and each time he received **absolution**, he was strengthened to continue his journey toward God.

During one such period of intense struggle, Silouan was blessed with a vision of **Christ**. In the vision, Christ told him, **"Keep your mind in hell and despair not."** This paradoxical instruction taught Silouan to embrace humility, recognize his dependence on God's grace, and persevere in the face of temptation. Through **repentance, confession, prayer, and spiritual warfare**, Silouan advanced on the path toward **theosis—union with God.** His life demonstrates that confession is not merely a legal formality but a vital step on the journey of transformation into **the likeness of Christ**.

Understanding Theosis: Union with God as the Goal of Christian Life

Theosis is the process of becoming united with God, the ultimate goal of the Christian life. It is a **lifelong journey** of transformation, where the believer is increasingly conformed to the image and likeness of Christ. St. Athanasius of Alexandria summarized the heart of the Christian faith in one sentence:

"God became man so that man might become god."

This **"becoming god"** does not mean becoming divine by nature but rather sharing in **God's divine life** through His grace. Theosis is the **progressive restoration of the divine image** within us, lost through sin, and involves growing in love, holiness, and communion with God. It is made possible through **God's grace** and the believer's cooperation in faith and good works—a process called **synergy**.

Confession and Repentance as Essential Steps on the Path to Theosis

Sin obstructs the journey toward theosis by **separating the believer from God**. Confession and repentance are vital because they restore the soul to a state of **grace and communion** with God. Through confession, the believer acknowledges their sins and weaknesses, and **absolution releases them from the burdens of guilt and shame**, allowing them to progress toward spiritual healing and transformation.

The spiritual journey requires **constant repentance**. As St. Isaac the Syrian taught:

"This life has been given to you for repentance. Do not waste it on other things."

Each act of repentance is a step closer to **union with God**.

The Role of Spiritual Warfare in Theosis

The journey toward theosis involves **spiritual warfare**—a daily struggle against temptation, sin, and the forces of evil. As believers strive to grow in **virtue and holiness**, they face challenges that test their faith and perseverance. Confession is one of the most powerful tools in this battle, offering renewal and strength for the soul to continue the fight.

St. Paul reminds us of this constant struggle:

"For we do not wrestle against flesh and blood, but against the rulers, against the authorities, against the cosmic powers over this present darkness, against the

spiritual forces of evil in the heavenly places" (Ephesians 6:12).

Through confession and repentance, believers gain clarity about their weaknesses and are **fortified by grace** to resist temptation, grow in humility, and advance in the life of the Spirit.

Fasting and Prayer: Preparation for Confession and Theosis

Fasting and prayer are essential tools for spiritual growth, helping believers cultivate self-discipline and **attentiveness to God**. Fasting prepares the heart for repentance by teaching the believer to **deny selfish desires** and focus on **spiritual nourishment**.

The connection between **fasting, confession, and the Eucharist** is profound. Fasting fosters humility and encourages the believer to **examine their life honestly**, making confession more meaningful. The renewed soul, cleansed through confession and strengthened by fasting, is then ready to participate in the Eucharist, the **source and summit of the Christian life**, which nourishes the soul on the path of theosis.

The Therapeutic Nature of Confession in the Process of Theosis

The Orthodox Church teaches that **confession is not merely legal but therapeutic**. Sin is understood as a **wound to the soul**, and confession is a way to **heal those wounds**. The priest acts as a **spiritual physician**, offering absolution as well as guidance for spiritual growth.

Through confession, the believer gains **greater self-awareness** and learns how to combat their spiritual weaknesses. This process is not about guilt but about **restoration and renewal**. Each confession brings the soul closer to healing, allowing the believer to progress in the journey of theosis.

Orthodox and Protestant Views on Confession: A Key Difference

Many **Protestant traditions** emphasize that believers can confess their sins directly to God through personal prayer. While Orthodoxy agrees that personal prayer is important, it teaches that **sacramental confession offers a unique grace** that goes beyond personal prayer. In the sacrament, the priest acts as **Christ's representative**, offering both absolution and spiritual guidance.

The Protestant doctrine of **"Once Saved, Always Saved"** contrasts sharply with the Orthodox understanding of salvation as a **lifelong process**. While some Protestants believe that salvation is secured by a one-time profession of faith, Orthodoxy teaches that salvation requires **ongoing repentance, confession, participation in the sacraments, and growth in holiness**.

Comparison with Roman Catholic Confession: Similarities and Differences

Both **Orthodox and Roman Catholic** churches practice sacramental confession, but there are important differences in emphasis. Roman Catholicism often emphasizes the **judicial aspect** of confession, with the priest acting **in persona Christi** (in the person of Christ) to pronounce **forgiveness and pardon**.

In contrast, Orthodox Christianity emphasizes the **therapeutic nature of confession**, focusing on the **healing of the soul** and spiritual renewal. The Orthodox priest acts as a **living icon of Christ** and a spiritual guide, helping the penitent grow in the life of grace and advance toward theosis.

The Eucharist and Theosis: A Continuing Journey

The **Eucharist** plays a central role in the life of the Orthodox believer, nourishing the soul on the path of theosis. Participation in the Eucharist is **both the goal and the means** of the believer's journey toward union with God. Through the Eucharist, the believer receives the **Body and Blood of Christ**, which imparts grace and strengthens them for the spiritual journey.

However, believers must **approach the Eucharist with a pure heart**, made ready through **confession and repentance**. The Eucharist is not merely a ritual but a **real encounter with Christ**, deepening the believer's union with Him and advancing them on the path of theosis.

Chapter 13. Concluding Prayer

O Lord Jesus Christ, who desires that all Your children grow in union with You, grant us the grace to confess our sins with humility and faith. Heal the wounds of our souls and strengthen us for the journey of theosis. Help us to persevere in spiritual warfare, discipline our desires through fasting, and prepare our hearts to receive You in the Eucharist. Through the prayers of St. Silouan the Athonite and all the saints, may we grow in Your likeness

and come to share in the joy of Your eternal Kingdom.
Now and ever, and unto ages of ages. Amen.

Chapter 13. Chapter Review Questions

What is the ultimate goal of the Christian life in Orthodox theology?

- o A) Moral perfection
- o B) Theosis—union with God
- o C) Material prosperity
- o D) Social recognition
- o **Correct Answer**: B) Theosis—union with God

What is the role of repentance in theosis?

- o A) It is unnecessary after baptism
- o B) It restores the believer's relationship with God and advances them toward union with Him
- o C) It replaces participation in the sacraments
- o D) It guarantees sinless living

How does Orthodox Confession differ from Protestant practice?

- o A) Orthodox Confession is private, while Protestants confess publicly

- o   B) Orthodox Confession involves a priest offering absolution and guidance, while Protestants emphasize personal prayer for forgiveness
- o   C) Orthodox Confession is optional
- o   D) Protestants fast before confession

What is the therapeutic nature of Confession?

- o   A) It heals the soul and restores inner peace
- o   B) It serves as a legal requirement
- o   C) It ensures perfection
- o   D) It replaces the need for fasting

What role does the Eucharist play in theosis?

- o   A) It guarantees salvation without repentance
- o   B) It nourishes the soul and strengthens the believer on the path to union **with God**
- o   C) It replaces confession
- o   D) It is only symbolic

Chapter 14

The Eucharist—Nourishment for Eternal Life, Liturgical Order, Icons, Hymns, Fasting, Entrances, and the Veneration of Saints

The Eucharist as the Central Sacrament of Orthodox Christianity -- The Central Sacrament of Spiritual Nourishment

A Story from the Life of St. Nektarios of Aegina: A Saint Who Hears Prayers

St. **Nektarios of Aegina** (1846–1920) is revered throughout the Orthodox Church for his humility, holiness, and miraculous intercession. After his death, countless pilgrims began visiting his tomb, praying for his intercession. Many reported healing miracles and spiritual comfort. One notable story involves a young woman who, plagued with illness, prayed to St. Nektarios from her hospital bed. That night, she dreamed of the saint visiting her, and upon waking, she found herself miraculously healed. This story is just one of many that demonstrate how **Orthodox saints, united with God, continue to hear the prayers of the faithful and intercede for them**.

Do Saints Hear Individual Prayers?

The Orthodox Church teaches that **saints are alive in Christ** and, through the grace of God, are aware of the needs of the faithful. While saints do not possess omniscience—an attribute reserved for God—they are

185

united with Him and participate in His divine knowledge to the extent He allows. As St. Paul writes:

"I am sure that neither death nor life, nor angels nor rulers, nor things present nor things to come, nor powers, nor height nor depth, nor anything else in all creation, will be able to separate us from the love of God in Christ Jesus our Lord" (Romans 8:38-39).

This unbroken communion means that the saints, though no longer on earth, **remain deeply connected to the Body of Christ**. Their intercession is an extension of God's love, and they can indeed hear the **individual prayers of the faithful** when those prayers are offered with humility and faith.

The saints are not mediators in place of Christ, but their prayers **join with ours** in the same way that believers on earth pray for one another. Asking for the intercession of a saint is like asking a trusted friend to pray for us—except that these friends now stand in the **presence of God**, perfected in holiness.

Do Icons Reflect Divine Reality?

Icons hold a central place in Orthodox worship, serving as **"windows to heaven."** They reflect the **divine reality** of the spiritual world and **make present the realities they**

depict. An icon is not just a picture or a religious art piece; it is a **sacramental medium** that allows believers to participate in the divine life.

The Theology of Icons

Icons depict Christ, the Theotokos, saints, and events from salvation history. They convey the truth that **God took on human flesh in Jesus Christ**, sanctifying matter and making it a vehicle for His presence. Because of the Incarnation, **matter is no longer separate from the spiritual**—it is capable of conveying divine grace. When believers venerate an icon, they are not worshipping the image itself but **honoring the reality it represents.** St. Basil the Great wrote:

"The honor paid to the image passes on to the prototype."

Thus, when a believer venerates an icon of Christ or a saint, that act of reverence reaches the **person depicted in the icon**, whether Christ or one of His holy ones. Icons are reminders that **heaven and earth are not distant** but intimately connected.

How the Saints Participate in the Divine Liturgy

During the Divine Liturgy, the Church teaches that the faithful on earth are joined by the **saints and angels in heaven**. This unity reflects the truth that **the Eucharist transcends time and space**, drawing together all of creation in worship of God. When the faithful ask for the intercession of saints during the liturgy, they are acknowledging this reality. The saints are not passive observers but **active participants**, praying for the Church and rejoicing in the Eucharistic offering.

The Small Entrance and Great Entrance: Signs of Heavenly Participation

- **The Small Entrance**, when the Gospel is brought in procession, signifies **Christ's presence among His people**, accompanied by the saints and angels.
- **The Great Entrance**, when the bread and wine are carried to the altar, symbolizes **Christ's journey to the Cross**. During this solemn procession, the Church invokes the prayers of the saints, recognizing that their intercession accompanies the offering of the gifts.

The Role of Icons and Hymns in Worship

Icons and hymns are essential elements in Orthodox worship, focusing the hearts and minds of the faithful on God.

- **Icons** reflect the reality of **God's presence** and the communion of saints. They are not merely decorative; they allow believers to connect spiritually with the saints and **the life of Christ**.
- **Hymns** chosen for the liturgy align with the themes of the season or feast day, guiding the faithful in prayer. Hymns often invoke the saints, reminding worshippers that they **pray alongside the Church** in heaven.

The Eucharist, Theosis, and Union with God

The **Eucharist is the ultimate sacrament of spiritual nourishment**, drawing believers closer to **theosis**—union with God. Through the Eucharist, believers receive the **Body and Blood of Christ**, participating in His divine life. The saints, having already attained union with God, join in this act of worship, rejoicing that the faithful on earth are also being transformed into the likeness of Christ.

Fasting Before the Eucharist: Preparing the Soul

Orthodox Christians fast before receiving the Eucharist to **prepare body and soul** for this sacred encounter. Fasting cultivates humility and **heightens spiritual awareness**, ensuring that believers approach the Eucharist with reverence and gratitude. Traditionally, fasting begins at **midnight** before the Divine Liturgy, reflecting the priority of **spiritual nourishment over physical needs**.

Spiritual Preparation for the Eucharist

Beyond fasting, Orthodox Christians prepare for the Eucharist through **prayer, confession, and reflection**. They are encouraged to examine their conscience and **receive absolution** before participating in the sacrament, ensuring they are spiritually ready. The Eucharist nourishes the soul, but it also requires believers to **cooperate with God's grace**, growing daily in holiness.

CHAPTER 14. Concluding Prayer

O Lord Jesus Christ, through the prayers of Your holy saints, unite us in worship and draw us closer to Your divine life. Help us to honor Your presence in the Eucharist and prepare our hearts through prayer, fasting, and repentance. Grant that we may be nourished by Your Body and Blood and grow in union with You, now and ever, and unto ages of ages. Amen.

CHAPTER 14. Review Questions

What is the Orthodox understanding of the intercession of saints?

- o A) Saints replace Christ as mediators
- o B) Saints participate in Christ's ministry and pray for the faithful
- o C) Saints are distant observers
- o D) Saints only intercede during feast days

How do icons reflect divine reality?

- o A) They are symbolic representations of God's presence
- o B) They serve as windows to heaven, making spiritual realities present
- o C) They are historical artifacts
- o D) They are decorative art pieces

What does the Great Entrance signify?

- o   A) The arrival of the priest
- o   B) Christ's journey to the Cross
- o   C) The arrival of the congregation
- o   D) The opening of the church doors

Why do Orthodox Christians fast before receiving the Eucharist?

- o   A) To earn merit
- o   B) To prepare body and soul for encountering Christ
- o   C) To fulfill a requirement
- o   D) To impress others

How do saints participate in the Divine Liturgy?

- o   A) They watch silently from heaven
- o   B) They join in the worship and offer intercession for the faithful
- o   C) They attend only on feast days
- o   D) They are remembered but do not participate

Chapter 15

Spiritual Warfare, Theosis, and the Transforming Power of Grace in Orthodox Christianity

The Christian Life as Spiritual Warfare and Theosis

A Story from the Life of St. Dionysius the Areopagite: Witnessing the Angels in Worship

St. **Dionysius the Areopagite**, a disciple of the Apostle Paul, described in his writings the **hierarchy of angels** and their participation in divine worship. He explained that the **angels constantly praise God** in the heavenly realms and join the faithful on earth during the celebration of the Divine Liturgy. St. Dionysius taught that the **earthly liturgy mirrors the heavenly worship** and that believers on earth participate with the **angels, archangels, and all heavenly beings** in glorifying God. His mystical writings remind us that the **Divine Liturgy is not confined to time and space**—it is an act of worship that unites heaven and earth.

How Angels Participate in the Divine Liturgy

Orthodox Christianity teaches that during the **Divine Liturgy**, angels are not passive observers but **active participants**, joining their voices with the faithful in worship. The **sanctuary, the altar, and the entire space of**

the church become a sacred meeting point where the earthly and heavenly realms converge.

- **Angels as Worshippers**: The angelic hosts glorify God continually, singing, **"Holy, Holy, Holy, Lord of Hosts; heaven and earth are full of Your glory"** (Isaiah 6:3). This angelic hymn, also known as the **Sanctus**, is echoed during the Divine Liturgy, inviting believers to join the heavenly chorus.

- **The Cherubic Hymn**: One of the most profound moments in the Divine Liturgy is the singing of the **Cherubic Hymn**, which proclaims:

"Let us who mystically represent the cherubim, and who sing the thrice-holy hymn to the life-creating Trinity, now lay aside all earthly cares."

This hymn reminds the faithful that **the Church on earth represents the cherubim**, worshipping alongside the angels and offering praise to God.

- **Angels as Intercessors**: During the liturgy, the priest invokes the **intercession of angels**, asking for their prayers on behalf of the Church. Angels are believed to accompany believers in worship and **carry their prayers to the throne of God**.

The Divine Liturgy teaches us that **heaven and earth are not separate realms** but are joined together in the worship of God, where angels and humans unite in a single act of praise.

Hesychastic Prayers for Beginners: The Jesus Prayer and Inner Stillness

Hesychasm is a **spiritual tradition in Orthodox Christianity** focused on inner stillness, contemplation, and direct experience of God's presence. For beginners, the **Jesus Prayer**—"Lord Jesus Christ, Son of God, have mercy on me, a sinner"—is the primary tool for entering into the Hesychastic way of prayer.

The Jesus Prayer: A Simple Yet Powerful Prayer

The Jesus Prayer is easy to learn but holds **profound spiritual depth**. By repeating the prayer slowly and attentively, believers focus their minds and hearts on **Christ**, setting aside distractions and cultivating inner stillness. The goal of the Jesus Prayer is not only to ask for mercy but to bring the soul into **constant awareness of God's presence**.

- **How to Begin**: Start by saying the Jesus Prayer **slowly and intentionally**. Beginners may begin with **a few minutes each day**, gradually increasing the time spent in prayer.

- **Breathing Techniques**: Some spiritual guides recommend coordinating the prayer with the breath. For example, breathe in while saying, **"Lord Jesus Christ, Son of God,"** and breathe out while saying, **"have mercy on me, a sinner."**

This rhythm helps calm the mind and **directs the heart toward God**.

The Role of Hesychasm in Spiritual Growth

Hesychastic prayer is not merely about quieting the mind but about **opening the heart to God's grace**. Through persistent practice, the believer learns to **combat distractions, temptations, and negative thoughts**—all of which are aspects of spiritual warfare. The ultimate goal of Hesychasm is **theosis**, where the believer becomes united with God through divine grace.

How Icons Aid Hesychastic Prayer

Icons play an important role in **Orthodox prayer life**. For beginners, **praying before an icon** can help focus the heart and mind on God. An icon is not just an artistic representation but a **window into divine reality**—a reminder of the presence of Christ, the Theotokos, or the saints.

When practicing **Hesychastic prayer**, the believer may place an icon in front of them to **keep their mind focused** on the presence of God. Praying with an icon is an acknowledgment that **heaven and earth are connected**, and through prayer, believers participate in that divine connection.

Prayer Ropes: Tools for Unceasing Prayer

Prayer ropes, similar to Rosaries, are an essential tool in the practice of **unceasing prayer**. Traditionally made of knotted wool or silk, prayer ropes help the faithful **maintain focus and consistency** while praying the Jesus Prayer.

- **How to Use a Prayer Rope**: Each knot on the rope marks one repetition of the Jesus Prayer. The rhythmic use of the prayer rope helps the believer stay attentive, especially during longer prayer sessions.
- **Practical Benefits**: For beginners, the prayer rope serves as a helpful guide, preventing the mind from wandering and ensuring that prayer remains **focused and intentional**.

**The Armor of God: Spiritual Protection in the
Battle Against Evil**

In Ephesians 6:10-18, St. Paul describes the **Armor of
God**, which provides believers with **spiritual protection** in
the battle against sin and temptation. The elements of the
Armor of God include:

- **The belt of truth**: Anchoring believers in God's
  truth.
- **The breastplate of righteousness**: Guarding the
  heart with integrity and holiness.
- **The shield of faith**: Defending against the attacks
  of doubt and despair.
- **The helmet of salvation**: Protecting the mind with
  the assurance of God's grace.
- **The sword of the Spirit**: The Word of God, used to
  combat lies and falsehood.

Hesychastic prayer, fasting, and confession strengthen
the soul, equipping believers to **put on the Armor of God**
and remain faithful in spiritual warfare.

Victory in Christ: Assurance of Triumph Over Sin and Death

The Orthodox faith teaches that **Christ has already triumphed** over sin and death through His resurrection. However, believers must actively **participate in that victory** by remaining vigilant in prayer, fasting, and repentance. Victory in spiritual warfare is not achieved by human effort alone but through **God's grace working within** the faithful.

Through the **Eucharist, prayer, and participation in the life of the Church**, believers are empowered to walk the path of theosis and grow in union with God.

Chapter 15. Concluding Prayer

O Lord Jesus Christ, You have surrounded us with Your holy angels and equipped us for the battle against sin. Teach us to pray without ceasing and to guard our hearts through the Jesus Prayer and inner stillness. Help us to focus our hearts on You, and through the intercession of Your angels and saints, may we grow in grace and walk the path of theosis. Now and ever, and unto ages of ages. Amen.

Chapter 15. Review Questions

What is the primary role of angels in the Divine Liturgy?

- A) They observe from a distance
- B) They actively participate in worship and offer intercession for the faithful
- C) They only attend on feast days
- D) They replace the priest in worship

What is the purpose of the Jesus Prayer?

- A) To replace the need for the Eucharist
- B) To focus the heart on Christ and cultivate inner stillness
- C) To earn merit
- D) To fulfill a fasting obligation

How do prayer ropes aid in prayer?

- A) They serve as good luck charms
- B) They help maintain focus and consistency in the practice of unceasing prayer
- C) They replace the need for confession
- D) They are purely decorative

What does the Cherubic Hymn remind the faithful of?

- o A) The importance of fasting
- o B) That the Church on earth joins the angels in worship
- o C) The arrival of the saints
- o D) The need for personal prayer

What is the goal of Hesychastic prayer?

- o A) To achieve mystical experiences
- o B) To cultivate inner stillness and grow in theosis
- o C) To fulfill a religious duty
- o D) To earn rewards

Chapter 16:

The Role of Sacraments in Orthodox Christianity and Their Connection to Theosis

The Sacraments as Pathways to the Divine Life

A Story from the Life of St. Seraphim of Sarov: The Power of Grace Through the Sacraments

St. **Seraphim of Sarov** (1754–1833), one of the most beloved saints of the Orthodox Church, was known for his holiness, miracles, and profound teachings on the **grace of the Holy Spirit**. He frequently ministered to people from all walks of life, encouraging them to seek transformation through the sacraments. One of his well-known encounters involved a conversation with a young nobleman, during which St. Seraphim explained the importance of receiving the **Eucharist, confession, and the gift of the Holy Spirit through Chrismation**. He emphasized that **divine grace is essential for the Christian life** and that it is through the sacraments that believers are empowered to **pursue theosis**.

The Role of the Sacraments in Grace: Can They Work Outside Orthodoxy?

The Orthodox Church teaches that **the sacraments are channels of divine grace**, instituted by Christ and administered within the life of the Church. However, the question of whether the sacraments can work outside of Orthodoxy is both **complex** and deeply tied to the understanding of **sacramental validity** and the **nature of the Church**.

Sacramental Validity Outside Orthodoxy

Orthodox Christianity recognizes that **God's grace is not limited by the boundaries of the Church**. While the fullness of the sacraments and the path to theosis are available within the Orthodox Church, there are circumstances in which **elements of grace may be present** outside Orthodoxy. For example:

- **Baptism**: The Orthodox Church acknowledges the validity of **Trinitarian baptism** (in the name of the Father, Son, and Holy Spirit) performed outside of Orthodoxy, though individuals may need to be formally received into the Church through **Chrismation**.

- **Marriage**: Orthodox Christians who marry non-Orthodox partners may still receive the **grace of marriage**, though such marriages ideally take place within the Church.

- **Confession and Eucharist**: The Orthodox Church teaches that the **Eucharist and confession** are tied directly to the life of the Church and **cannot be fully experienced** outside the sacramental community governed by **apostolic succession**.

While **some grace may be present** in non-Orthodox sacraments, the Orthodox Church teaches that the **fullness of divine grace**—especially as it pertains to the path of theosis—can only be found within the life of the **One, Holy, Catholic, and Apostolic Church**.

Chrismation vs. Confirmation: Key Differences

While **Chrismation** in Orthodoxy and **Confirmation** in Roman Catholicism may appear similar, there are essential theological and practical differences between the two.

The Timing and Theology

- **Chrismation**: In the Orthodox Church, Chrismation is typically performed **immediately after baptism** (including infant baptism). It signifies the **sealing of the Holy Spirit**, empowering the believer for the Christian journey from the very beginning. Through Chrismation, the individual is fully incorporated into the life of the Church and is given the **grace needed for spiritual growth and participation in the sacraments**.

- **Confirmation**: In Roman Catholicism, Confirmation is usually administered **at a later age**, often during adolescence, as a way of affirming the **individual's commitment** to the faith. It is considered a "coming of age" sacrament, marking the individual's personal decision to embrace their baptismal faith.

The Holy Spirit and Empowerment

Chrismation emphasizes the **gift of the Holy Spirit as a continuous presence** in the life of the believer, empowering them for **spiritual warfare, ministry, and participation in the sacraments**. In Roman Catholicism, Confirmation also emphasizes the Holy Spirit, but with a focus on **personal commitment** and maturity within the faith.

Orthodoxy holds that Chrismation is an **integral part of initiation** into the Christian life, inseparable from baptism. In contrast, Confirmation in Catholicism functions more as a **completion of initiation** that is distinct from baptism.

The Eucharist: The Source and Summit of Christian Life

The **Eucharist** is the **heart of Orthodox worship**, where believers receive the **Body and Blood of Christ**, nourishing their souls and drawing them deeper into **union with God**. Orthodox theology emphasizes that the Eucharist is not merely symbolic but is the **Real Presence of Christ**, sustaining believers on their path to theosis.

Because the Eucharist is intimately connected with the **life of the Church**, it cannot be fully separated from the sacramental community. For this reason, the Orthodox Church practices **closed communion**, meaning that only those who are properly prepared and in communion with the Church may receive the Eucharist. This practice is not meant to exclude, but to **honor the sacredness of the sacrament** and ensure that participants receive it with the necessary faith and preparation.

Confession: Healing and Renewal Through Repentance

Confession is a sacrament of **healing and renewal**, offering believers a way to overcome sin, receive forgiveness, and experience spiritual renewal. Through the grace imparted in confession, believers are strengthened to resist future temptations and **continue their journey toward theosis**.

In Orthodoxy, confession is viewed not merely as a legal act but as a **therapeutic encounter**. The priest, acting as a **spiritual physician**, helps guide the penitent toward healing and transformation.

Marriage: A Path to Theosis Through Mutual Love and Self-Giving

Marriage is a sacrament in which husband and wife become **one flesh**, reflecting the **union of Christ with His Church**. Through mutual love, self-sacrifice, and faithfulness, the couple grows in holiness, helping one another on the path to **theosis**. The grace of marriage strengthens the couple to **bear each other's burdens** and cultivate a life of **virtue and love**.

Holy Orders: The Sacrament of Apostolic Ministry

Holy Orders is the sacrament through which individuals are **ordained to serve the Church** as deacons, priests, or bishops. Through ordination, clergy receive the grace needed to **minister the sacraments** and shepherd the faithful. The continuation of **apostolic succession** ensures that the Church remains connected to the ministry of the Apostles and preserves the **authentic teachings of Christ**.

Anointing of the Sick: Physical and Spiritual Healing

The sacrament of **anointing the sick** provides both **physical and spiritual healing**. Through the anointing with holy oil, the sick receive **divine grace** to strengthen them in their suffering and prepare their souls for eternal life. Even if physical healing is not granted, the sacrament offers **spiritual renewal and comfort**, reminding believers that they are never abandoned by God.

The Purifying Power of Grace: Transformation Through the Sacraments

Each sacrament imparts **grace that purifies and transforms** the believer, cleansing the soul from sin and drawing the individual closer to God. This grace is not static but requires the **active cooperation** of the believer, who must strive to live according to the teachings of Christ.

Sacramental Life and Theosis: Union with God Through Grace

The **sacramental life** is essential to the pursuit of **theosis**—the process of becoming one with God. Each sacrament plays a role in **healing the soul, strengthening the believer**, and fostering communion with Christ. Through the sacraments, believers are continually renewed and empowered to walk the **narrow path of salvation**, growing in holiness and love.

Chapter 16. Concluding Prayer

O Lord Jesus Christ, through Your holy sacraments, You have given us the grace to grow in Your likeness. Strengthen us through baptism, chrismation, confession, the Eucharist, and all the sacraments, that we may walk the path of theosis and grow in union with You. Help us to love one another, persevere in faith, and serve You with joy. Now and ever, and unto ages of ages. Amen.

Chapter 16. Review Questions

What is the primary difference between Chrismation and Confirmation?

- ○ A) Chrismation emphasizes the gift of the Holy Spirit, while Confirmation emphasizes personal maturity
- ○ B) Chrismation is administered immediately after baptism, while Confirmation is given at a later age
- ○ C) Chrismation is optional, while Confirmation is required
- ○ D) Chrismation and Confirmation are identical in theology and practice

What is the purpose of confession in Orthodox Christianity?

- ○ A) To provide legal absolution
- ○ B) To offer healing, renewal, and grace for spiritual growth
- ○ C) To replace prayer
- ○ D) To fulfill a ritual obligation

Can sacraments outside of Orthodoxy provide grace?

- A) No, they are entirely invalid
- B) Some sacraments, such as baptism, may convey grace if performed in a Trinitarian manner
- C) Only if the person is Orthodox
- D) All sacraments outside Orthodoxy are equally valid

What is the purpose of the Eucharist in Orthodox Christianity?

- A) It is a symbolic meal
- B) It unites believers with Christ and nourishes the soul for the journey of theosis
- C) It guarantees salvation
- D) It replaces the need for confession

Chapter 17

Mariology in Orthodoxy

The Theological Significance of the Theotokos

A Story from the Life of St. Gregory Palamas: A Vision of the Theotokos

St. **Gregory Palamas** (1296–1359), the great theologian of Hesychasm, experienced a vision of the **Theotokos** during his ascetic life on Mount Athos. The Virgin Mary, bathed in divine light, appeared to him as he prayed in stillness, blessing his efforts and assuring him of her **intercession**. This experience strengthened Palamas, leading him to deepen his understanding of **prayer, theosis, and God's grace**. His encounter with the Theotokos also reflected the Orthodox belief that Mary **actively participates** in the life of the Church, offering her help to those who seek God through humility, prayer, and repentance.

Marian Apparitions in Orthodox Theology: A Cautious Approach

In Orthodox Christianity, **Marian apparitions**—instances where believers claim to have seen or encountered the Theotokos—are treated with both **reverence and caution**. While the Church acknowledges that the Virgin Mary can appear to believers, such experiences are approached carefully to discern whether they are **authentic encounters with divine grace** or

deceptions. The Church's focus is always on **humility, spiritual growth, and discernment**, ensuring that visions align with the **teachings of the Apostles and the Church Fathers**.

Orthodoxy differs from Roman Catholicism in its approach to Marian apparitions. While the Catholic Church has **formally approved** several apparitions—such as those at **Lourdes and Fatima**—Orthodoxy is **more reserved** about granting official recognition to such events. This is rooted in the belief that **visions and signs** are secondary to the **spiritual life grounded in prayer, the sacraments, and the teachings of the Church**. Apparitions, even if genuine, are seen as **personal gifts of grace**, not essential to the faith.

Criteria for Authenticity in Orthodox Christianity

The Orthodox Church evaluates claimed Marian apparitions through a process of **discernment**, considering whether the apparition:

1. **Affirms Orthodox doctrine**: The content of the apparition must align with the teachings of the Church and the Gospel.
2. **Encourages humility and repentance**: True apparitions lead to greater **devotion to Christ** and

the pursuit of **holiness** through the sacraments and prayer.

3. **Avoids sensationalism or pride**: Authentic visions draw believers closer to God without glorifying the visionary or the event itself.

4. **Bears spiritual fruit**: A genuine apparition inspires **love, faith, repentance, and increased participation in the sacramental life** of the Church.

Orthodox theology emphasizes that **visions and miracles** are not the primary means through which believers encounter God. Instead, **prayer, fasting, confession, and the Eucharist** remain the central ways to grow in the life of faith.

Notable Examples of Marian Apparitions in Orthodox Tradition

While the Orthodox Church does not emphasize apparitions as much as the Roman Catholic Church, several well-known instances of **Marian appearances** are honored within Orthodoxy.

The Protection of the Theotokos (The Feast of Pokrov)

One of the most beloved examples of a Marian apparition is the **Protection of the Theotokos**, which is celebrated on **October 1st** in the Orthodox Church. According to tradition, during a siege of Constantinople in the 10th century, the Virgin Mary appeared in the church of **Blachernae**, spreading her veil (omophorion) over the city as a sign of **protection**. This vision gave the people courage, and the city was spared from destruction. The **Feast of Pokrov** commemorates the Virgin Mary's **constant care and intercession** for the Church.

The Apparition of the Theotokos on Mount Athos

Mount Athos, often referred to as the **Garden of the Theotokos**, has long been associated with the Virgin Mary. According to tradition, Mary appeared to a group of monks, blessing the monastic community and assuring them of her **special protection** over Mount Athos. This vision reflects the Orthodox understanding that the Theotokos is a **spiritual mother** who offers guidance and comfort to those seeking God through prayer and asceticism.

Comparison with Roman Catholic Marian Apparitions

While both **Orthodoxy and Roman Catholicism** believe in the possibility of Marian apparitions, there are key differences in how these events are understood and treated.

1. **Theological Context**
    - **Roman Catholicism** places significant emphasis on certain Marian apparitions, granting them **formal approval** and incorporating their messages into popular devotion and theology. Apparitions like those at **Fatima, Lourdes, and Guadalupe** have become central to Catholic spirituality.
    - **Orthodoxy** sees visions as **personal spiritual experiences** rather than universal revelations. The focus remains on the **sacramental life** and the **teachings of the Church**, with the belief that **salvation comes through participation in the Eucharist, prayer, and repentance**, not through visions.

2. **Messages of Apparitions**

   o   Roman Catholic apparitions often carry specific messages—such as calls for **penance, prayer, and devotion**—sometimes introducing new devotions like the **Rosary** or the **First Saturdays devotion**.

   o   In Orthodoxy, any message from an apparition must align fully with **Apostolic teaching**. The Church does not develop new devotions or dogmas based on apparitions. Instead, such experiences are understood as **encouragements to return to Christ** through existing spiritual practices.

3. **Discernment of Visions**

   o   Roman Catholicism has a formal process for approving apparitions, involving investigation and recognition by Church authorities.

   o   Orthodox Christianity is **less institutionalized** in this regard, leaving the discernment of apparitions to **spiritual fathers and bishops**, with a focus on whether the vision promotes **humility and repentance**.

The Role of Marian Apparitions in Orthodox Spiritual Life

Marian apparitions, when considered authentic, are viewed as **gifts of grace** that strengthen the faithful in their journey toward **theosis**. The purpose of such visions is not to add new revelations but to **reawaken devotion to Christ** and the **sacramental life of the Church**. Orthodox Christians are reminded that, while visions and miracles are possible, **the path to salvation lies in humility, repentance, and participation in the sacraments**.

Orthodox Marian Prayers and Hymns

The deep devotion to the Theotokos in Orthodoxy is expressed through prayers and hymns. Even without apparitions, the faithful regularly turn to her in prayer, knowing that she intercedes on their behalf. Examples of Orthodox Marian prayers include:

- **The Akathist Hymn**:
"Rejoice, O Bride Unwedded!"
- **The Paraklesis to the Theotokos**:
"O most holy Theotokos, intercede for us!"

These prayers reflect the central role of the Theotokos in Orthodox spirituality, offering believers a way to **draw closer to Christ** through her intercession.

Chapter 17. Concluding Prayer

O Most Holy Theotokos, ever-virgin and full of grace, guide us on the path of salvation. Whether through your appearances or your constant prayers, lead us to your Son, our Lord Jesus Christ. Teach us to walk in humility, to seek repentance, and to grow in faith. Now and ever, and unto ages of ages. Amen.

Chapter17. Review Questions

How does Orthodox Christianity approach Marian apparitions?

- o A) It rejects all visions as false.
- o B) It approaches them with reverence and caution, emphasizing discernment and alignment with Apostolic teaching.
- o C) It formalizes and approves new devotions based on them.
- o D) It encourages sensationalism

What is the significance of the Feast of Pokrov?

- o A) It celebrates Mary's birth.
- o B) It commemorates the Theotokos' protection over Constantinople.
- o C) It celebrates Mary's Assumption.
- o D) It marks the founding of the Church.

How does Orthodoxy differ from Roman Catholicism regarding Marian apparitions?

- o A) Orthodoxy treats them as personal experiences rather than universal revelations.
- o B) Orthodoxy formalizes them as new dogmas.
- o C) Orthodoxy rejects all apparitions.
- o D) Orthodoxy introduces new devotions through apparitions.

What is the purpose of Marian apparitions in Orthodox theology?

- o A) To develop new doctrines.
- o B) To encourage devotion to Christ and deepen participation in the sacramental life.
- o C) To replace Church teaching.
- o D) To provide entertainment.

Chapter 18:

Conclusion – Embracing
Authentic Faith
Through Western Orthodoxy

A Reflection: St. Nicholas and the Pursuit of Authentic Faith

St. **Nicholas of Myra**, known as the Wonderworker, provides an example of what it means to pursue **authentic faith**. His life was marked by both **fierce defense of truth** and profound **compassion** for the poor and suffering. At the Council of Nicaea in 325 AD, Nicholas defended the true nature of Christ, confronting heresy without compromise. At the same time, he was known for **generous acts of mercy**, secretly providing dowries to impoverished families and freeing prisoners from unjust punishment.

St. Nicholas exemplifies the balance that **Western Orthodoxy** seeks to cultivate—a faith that is rooted in **truth, love, and sacramental life**. His legacy reminds us that **authentic faith** is not just a matter of doctrine but is lived through **humility, service, and participation in the grace of God**.

The Journey into Western Orthodoxy: A Path to Authentic Faith

This book has explored the rich theological heritage of **Western Orthodoxy** and its distinct path toward **authentic Christian faith**. In the face of **modern relativism, shifting doctrines, and cultural confusion**, Western Orthodoxy

226

offers a stable and **uncompromising foundation** grounded in the **faith of the Apostles, the Church Fathers, and the ancient councils**. It is a path that draws believers into deeper communion with God through the **sacraments, liturgy, prayer, and spiritual discipline**.

The goal of this exploration is not merely to inform but to **invite**. It is an invitation to reflect deeply on the teachings of Christ and His Church and to consider how **faith is most authentically lived out today**. Western Orthodoxy stands as both a **reminder and a call**—a reminder of the unchanging truths entrusted to the Church from the beginning and a call to embrace the **narrow path** of salvation with courage and love.

The Role of the Sacraments in the Journey of Faith

Central to this journey are the **sacraments**, which serve as **channels of divine grace** and the means by which believers participate in **the life of God**. As we have explored, the sacraments are not mere rituals but transformative encounters with **Christ Himself**. Through **Baptism**, believers are united with Christ in His death and resurrection; in **Chrismation**, they are sealed with the Holy Spirit. The **Eucharist** nourishes the soul with the very

Body and Blood of Christ, drawing believers into union with Him. **Confession** offers healing and renewal through repentance, while **Marriage, Holy Orders, and Anointing of the Sick** provide grace for the specific vocations and challenges of life.

These sacraments sustain the faithful on the journey toward **theosis**—the process of becoming **one with God**, transformed by His grace. It is through this participation in the sacramental life that believers are empowered to grow in holiness and reflect **Christ's love** to the world.

Orthodox Distinctives: A Faith Rooted in Tradition

Throughout this book, we have contrasted the teachings of **Western Orthodoxy** with those of **Roman Catholicism, Protestantism, and modernist ideologies**. While all Christian traditions share a desire to follow Christ, we have explored the importance of **preserving the original teachings** transmitted by the Apostles and the early Church.

- **Roman Catholicism** has developed doctrines over time—such as the **Immaculate Conception and Papal Infallibility**—that differ from Orthodox theology.

- **Protestantism**, in reaction to perceived abuses in Roman Catholicism, has often discarded essential elements of the faith, such as the **sacramental priesthood, the Eucharist, and the role of the saints**.

- **Western Orthodoxy** offers a **middle way**, preserving the ancient teachings of the undivided Church while expressing them through the **Western liturgical and spiritual traditions**. It invites believers to experience a faith that is both **deeply rooted in history and fully alive in the present**.

Faith and Spiritual Discipline: The Role of Theosis, Synergy, and Asceticism

One of the key themes of this book is the **Orthodox understanding of salvation as theosis**—the process of becoming **partakers of the divine nature** (2 Peter 1:4). Unlike views that see salvation as a one-time event, Orthodoxy teaches that salvation is a **lifelong journey** of transformation, requiring both **divine grace and human effort**. This **synergy** between God's grace and human will calls believers to actively **participate in their salvation** through prayer, repentance, and sacramental life.

We have also explored the importance of **asceticism**—spiritual disciplines such as fasting, prayer, and almsgiving—that help believers overcome the passions and grow in virtue. Far from being burdensome, these practices are **gifts** that guide the soul toward greater freedom and **deeper union with God**.

The Narrow Path: An Invitation to Walk in Truth and Love

Jesus taught that the path to salvation is narrow (Matthew 7:14), and **Western Orthodoxy embraces this truth**. It does not seek to conform to the changing values of the world but offers a **faithful witness** to the unchanging teachings of Christ. In a world that often promotes **moral and spiritual relativism**, Western Orthodoxy stands as a beacon of **truth, love, and stability**.

This faith is not a burden but a **gift**—an invitation to **encounter the living God** through His Church and to walk with Him in love. The teachings of Christ are not meant to restrict but to **free the soul** to grow in holiness and experience **true joy**.

A Call to Embrace the Life of the Church

This book was designed to serve as a **guide for inquirers into Western Orthodoxy**. It is meant to accompany a **16- to 18-week catechism course**, offering insights into the teachings, sacraments, and spiritual practices of the Church. However, it is not the end of the journey—it is an invitation to **take the next step**.

For those who feel drawn to the path of **Western Orthodoxy**, the Church extends an open hand. You are invited to join the **community of believers** who walk this ancient path, sharing in the life of Christ through the **Eucharist, prayer, and sacramental living**. The journey may not always be easy, but it is filled with **grace, love, and transformation**.

Chapte 18. Concluding Prayer

O Lord Jesus Christ, the Way, the Truth, and the Life, lead us on the narrow path to Your Kingdom. Strengthen us through Your sacraments, guide us with Your truth, and fill us with Your love. Through the prayers of the Theotokos and all the saints, may we grow in the grace of the Holy Spirit and walk faithfully with You, now and ever, and unto ages of ages. Amen.

Chapter 18. Review Questions

1. **What is the ultimate goal of the Christian life according to Orthodox theology?**
   - o A) To perform good works
   - o B) Theosis—becoming united with God
   - o C) To earn a place in heaven
   - o D) To escape suffering

2. **How do the sacraments function in Orthodox Christianity?**
   - o A) As symbols of religious obligation
   - o B) As channels of divine grace that transform believers
   - o C) As optional rites
   - o D) As substitutes for faith

What is the relationship between divine grace and human effort in Orthodox theology?

- o A) Synergy—salvation requires cooperation between God's grace and human free will
- o B) Salvation is entirely dependent on human effort
- o C) Salvation is purely a gift with no human participation
- o D) Grace only applies to clergy

Why does Western Orthodoxy emphasize the sacramental life?

- o A) To maintain tradition for its own sake
- o B) To provide the grace necessary for spiritual growth and transformation
- o C) To guarantee salvation
- o D) To separate itself from other traditions

What distinguishes Western Orthodoxy from Roman Catholicism and Protestantism?

- o A) Its rejection of all tradition
- o B) Its preservation of ancient teachings while expressing them in Western forms
- o C) Its focus on personal revelation over community worship
- o D) Its opposition to all other forms of Christianity

Western Orthodoxy offers a path rooted in the **ancient faith of the Apostles**, providing stability, love, and truth in a world that often seems lost. It invites every seeker to **embrace the life of the Church** and experience the **transforming power of God's grace**. The journey may be narrow, but it leads to **eternal joy in communion with God**.

Chapter 19:

Stories of Conversion to

Orthodoxy

The path to faith is rarely a straight line. It winds and bends through the complexities of life, often leading individuals through moments of doubt, questioning, and deep reflection. For those who find themselves drawn to the ancient traditions of Western Orthodoxy, the journey can be both challenging and profoundly transformative. It is a path filled with questions about identity, truth, and the nature of God, but it is also one that leads to a deep sense of belonging and peace.

Each person's journey is unique. Some are raised in religious households but, over time, grow disillusioned with the faith of their upbringing. Others start their journey with no religious background at all, relying solely on reason, science, or philosophy to make sense of the world. Still others may explore a variety of spiritual practices before finally encountering Orthodoxy, realizing that it offers a depth and richness that they had not found elsewhere. For many, the turning point comes when they experience the beauty and mystery of the Orthodox liturgy—a moment that awakens something deep within them, something that had long been dormant.

These stories of conversion to Western Orthodoxy are powerful illustrations of how God works in the lives of individuals, gently guiding them toward a deeper understanding of His love and truth. They show how people from all walks of life—scientists, philosophers, secular humanists, and spiritual wanderers—can come to realize that the fullness of life is not found in individual pursuits or intellectual mastery but in communion with the living God. These stories are about transformation, about leaving behind old ways of thinking and embracing a new life rooted in the teachings and practices of the Church.

In the chapters that follow, we will hear from individuals who have made this journey—some from staunchly secular backgrounds, others from deeply religious ones. Their experiences vary, but the common thread is the deep longing for truth, beauty, and a connection with something greater than themselves. Each story serves as a testament to the enduring appeal of Orthodoxy and its ability to address the deepest yearnings of the human heart.

These conversions are not merely intellectual or emotional shifts; they are holistic transformations. They involve not only the mind and the heart but also the body, as each person comes to understand the significance of the sacraments, particularly the Eucharist. The Orthodox Church offers a way of life that encompasses every aspect of being, from daily prayers to communal worship, from fasting to feasting, from repentance to theosis—the process of becoming one with God through His grace.

Through these stories, we see that the journey to Orthodoxy is not always easy. It requires humility, the willingness to question long-held beliefs, and often, a period of deep struggle. But for those who persevere, the reward is great: a sense of peace and purpose, a home in the Church, and a relationship with God that continues to deepen over time.

As we explore these conversion stories, may they serve as both inspiration and encouragement for those on their own spiritual journey. Whether you are just beginning to explore Orthodoxy or have been on the path for some time, these stories remind us that the journey to faith is ongoing and that God is always drawing us closer to Him, inviting us to participate in His divine life.

These narratives are not meant to present a formula for conversion, as every journey is distinct, shaped by individual experiences and circumstances. Instead, they offer glimpses into how the ancient truths of Orthodoxy continue to resonate with modern seekers, addressing their intellectual, spiritual, and existential questions in ways that no other tradition has. For many, Orthodoxy is the fulfillment of a long and arduous search for truth—a homecoming to a faith that is both ancient and alive, timeless and relevant.

As you read these stories, reflect on your own journey. Consider the ways in which God might be calling you deeper into His love and truth, and know that you are not alone. There are many who have walked this path before you, and their stories are a testament to the transforming power of God's grace.

The Philosopher's Dilemma

James had always been a thinker. From an early age, he found himself captivated by questions of existence, purpose, and the nature of reality. While most of his friends were absorbed in typical teenage interests, James spent his spare time reading the works of great philosophers—Plato, Aristotle, Descartes, Kant, Nietzsche—each offering a unique perspective on the meaning of life and the nature of truth. By the time he entered university, philosophy had become his passion, his guiding light. He was determined to find answers to the ultimate questions of life through the power of human reason.

James was not raised in a religious household. His parents were nominal Christians, attending church occasionally on major holidays but never pushing any particular belief system on him. As a result, religion had never played a significant role in his upbringing. By the time he reached adulthood, James had come to see faith as a crutch—something people turned to when they couldn't face the harsh realities of the world. For James, the only path to truth was through reason and logic.

As he pursued his philosophy degree, James became more entrenched in his secular worldview. He debated with fellow students and professors, challenging religious beliefs as outdated and irrational. He admired philosophers like Nietzsche, who proclaimed that "God is dead," and Sartre, who embraced the existential idea that life had no inherent meaning except the one individuals gave it. For James, the universe was a place of endless possibility but no ultimate purpose. Humans were free to create their own meaning in a world without divine guidance.

Despite his intellectual confidence, there was a growing restlessness inside James. The deeper he delved into philosophy, the more he realized that no system of thought—whether it was rationalism, existentialism, or materialism—could fully satisfy his longing for answers. Every philosopher he studied seemed to arrive at a different conclusion about the nature of reality, and the more questions he asked, the fewer answers he seemed to find. Life, it seemed, was full of contradictions, and human reason alone wasn't enough to resolve them.

After graduating with honors, James found himself at a crossroads. He had a prestigious academic career ahead of him, with opportunities to pursue graduate studies and perhaps even become a professor. But despite his achievements, the nagging sense of emptiness persisted. He had spent years seeking the truth, yet he felt no closer to it than when he had started. Late at night, he would sit in his study, surrounded by books, wondering if the answers he sought could ever truly be found.

One evening, while browsing the philosophy section of a local bookstore, James came across a book he had never noticed before: *The Mystical Theology of the Eastern Church* by Vladimir Lossky. Intrigued by the title and the subject matter—Eastern Orthodoxy—he picked it up and began flipping through the pages. The language was dense, filled with references to Church Fathers and theological concepts he had never studied before, but something about it drew him in. Lossky spoke of the mystery of God, of a divine reality that transcended human reason and could only be approached through faith and experience.

For the first time, James was confronted with the idea that human reason, while valuable, was limited in its ability to comprehend the fullness of truth. The Eastern Orthodox tradition, as Lossky described it, did not dismiss reason, but it recognized that there were aspects of reality that could not be fully grasped through intellectual means alone. There was a deeper, mystical dimension to life that could only be accessed through prayer, contemplation, and communion with God.

James was both fascinated and skeptical. He had spent his entire life relying on reason to navigate the world— could there really be another way of knowing? The idea that faith could offer a path to truth, one that went beyond the limits of human logic, was foreign to him. And yet, something about the book resonated deeply with the restlessness he had been feeling. There was a humility in the Orthodox approach to knowledge, a recognition that humans, finite and fallible, could not expect to fully comprehend the infinite mystery of God.

After finishing Lossky's book, James decided to explore Eastern Orthodoxy further. He read the works of the Church Fathers—St. Gregory of Nyssa, St. Athanasius, St. Maximus the Confessor—men whose philosophical depth was matched by their profound spirituality. These were not philosophers who tried to explain away the mysteries of existence through abstract reasoning. Rather, they embraced the mystery of God, acknowledging that while certain truths could be understood through reason, the ultimate truth could only be experienced through relationship with God.

Intrigued, James decided to visit a local Western Orthodox church. He wasn't entirely sure what he was looking for—perhaps just a glimpse into this ancient faith that seemed to offer answers to questions he had never thought to ask. As he entered the church, he was struck by the beauty and stillness of the space. Icons adorned the walls, flickering candles cast a warm glow, and the soft murmur of prayers filled the air. There was something sacred here, something that transcended the intellectual debates he had spent years immersed in.

The liturgy began, and James was immediately captivated by the ancient chants, the incense rising to the heavens, and the careful, deliberate movements of the clergy. There were no impassioned sermons or emotional appeals—just a deep, reverent worship of God. It was as if time stood still, and James found himself drawn into the mystery of the moment.

After the service, James met with Father Anthony, the priest, who welcomed him warmly. They spoke for a while about James's background in philosophy and his interest in Orthodoxy. James was surprised to find that Father Anthony was well-versed in philosophy and theology, able to engage with him on topics ranging from Plato to Nietzsche.

"I've spent my whole life searching for the truth," James admitted. "But the more I search, the more I realize how little I actually know. How can we claim to know anything about God, or about the ultimate nature of reality?"

Father Anthony smiled gently. "Orthodoxy doesn't claim to have all the answers. In fact, we embrace the mystery of God. Human reason can take us far, but it can only go so far. Faith doesn't contradict reason—it transcends it. God is not a puzzle to be solved but a Person to be known. And we come to know Him through the life of the Church, through prayer, and through the sacraments. It's not about intellectual mastery—it's about communion with the living God."

James pondered Father Anthony's words. For so long, he had equated knowledge with intellectual understanding. But here was a different kind of knowledge—a knowledge that came through experience, through relationship with the divine. It was humbling, and yet it felt like the missing piece he had been searching for all along.

Over the next few months, James began attending the Western Orthodox church regularly. He immersed himself in the prayers, the liturgy, and the teachings of the Church. He learned about the Orthodox concept of *theosis*—the process of becoming united with God through His grace. The more he studied, the more he realized that Orthodoxy offered a holistic vision of truth—one that embraced both reason and faith, both the mind and the heart.

The idea of *theosis* captivated James. In his philosophical studies, he had always sought to understand the nature of existence, but here was a faith that taught not just understanding, but transformation. Orthodoxy didn't just offer answers to philosophical questions—it offered a path to becoming more like Christ, to participating in the divine life.

Eventually, James made the decision to be chrismated into the Orthodox Church. It was a decision that felt both surprising and inevitable, as if all his years of philosophical searching had been leading him to this moment. On the day of his chrismation, as Father Anthony anointed him with holy oil, James felt a deep sense of peace. This was not the peace of having all the intellectual answers—those questions would never fully go away—but the peace of knowing that he didn't have to figure it all out on his own. He was part of something greater, something eternal, something that transcended the limits of human understanding.

In the months that followed, James's life took on a new depth. He continued to study philosophy, but now with a different perspective. He no longer saw reason and faith as being in opposition; rather, they worked together to point him toward the truth. His prayers became more focused, and he found joy in the daily rhythm of the Orthodox spiritual life. The restlessness that had once driven him to seek answers in books and theories had been replaced by a sense of belonging—a sense that he had found his true home in the mystery of God.

James's journey from secular philosophy to Orthodoxy wasn't about abandoning his love for reason. It was about realizing that reason alone was not enough. The deepest truths of existence couldn't be grasped through intellectual effort alone—they had to be received, experienced, and lived. And in the Orthodox Church, James had found the fullness of those truths, the path that led beyond reason to the infinite mystery of God.

The Scientist's Discovery

    Dr. Sarah had always been a person of reason. As a child, she was drawn to the natural world, endlessly fascinated by its complexities and wonders. Her love for science only deepened as she grew older, and by the time she entered university, she was fully committed to a life of research. With a Ph.D. in immunology, Sarah had built a respected career in medical research, dedicating herself to understanding how the human body worked at the cellular level. For Sarah, science was not only her profession but her guiding light—a lens through which she made sense of the world.

    Sarah had been raised in a loosely religious household, with her parents attending church occasionally, more out of tradition than genuine belief. By the time Sarah reached adulthood, faith had become a distant memory, something that seemed unnecessary in the face of scientific progress. She saw religion as a relic of the past, a set of myths and superstitions that provided comfort to those unwilling to face the cold realities of the universe. For Sarah, the beauty and order of the natural world were explained through biology, physics, and chemistry. There was no need to believe in something beyond what could be observed, measured, and quantified.

Despite her professional success, Sarah couldn't shake a persistent sense of longing. Though she would never have admitted it to her colleagues, there were moments when she felt an emptiness that science couldn't fill. Late at night, after long hours spent in the lab, she sometimes found herself staring out the window at the stars, wondering if there was more to life than the mechanics of biology. But those thoughts were quickly dismissed as irrational. She was a scientist, after all—her world was grounded in evidence, not in the speculation of something beyond it.

Everything changed one afternoon during a casual conversation with a colleague, Dr. Peter Novak, who also happened to be an Orthodox Christian. Sarah had always admired Peter's calm demeanor and thoughtful approach to both work and life. They were discussing a particularly challenging research problem when Peter casually mentioned something about his faith.

"I find it fascinating," Peter said, "how the complexity of the immune system mirrors the beauty and order that's inherent in creation. For me, it's hard not to see the hand of God in the intricate design of life."

Sarah was taken aback. She hadn't realized that Peter was religious, and the idea that someone as intelligent and accomplished as him could believe in God challenged her assumptions. Intrigued, she asked, "You're really religious? But how do you reconcile that with being a scientist? Doesn't faith contradict everything we know about the natural world?"

Peter smiled and shook his head. "Not at all. In Orthodoxy, faith and science aren't at odds. They're different ways of seeking truth. Science helps us understand the 'how' of creation, but faith helps us understand the 'why.' The more I learn about the natural world, the more it deepens my sense of awe and wonder for the Creator. There's room for both reason and faith in the human experience."

Sarah had heard similar sentiments before, but for some reason, hearing it from Peter gave her pause. He wasn't defensive or dogmatic, and he wasn't trying to convert her. He simply seemed at peace with both his faith and his scientific work, something Sarah couldn't quite understand. For her, there had always been a sharp divide between reason and religion.

A few weeks later, Peter invited Sarah to attend a Western Orthodox liturgy. He assured her that there would be no pressure to participate—it would simply be an opportunity to observe a tradition that had been practiced for centuries. Sarah, still skeptical but intrigued, agreed to go. At the very least, it would be an interesting cultural experience.

The moment Sarah stepped into the church, she was struck by the profound sense of reverence that filled the space. The soft glow of candlelight, the smell of incense, and the quiet murmur of prayers created an atmosphere of sacredness that felt almost otherworldly. As the liturgy began, Sarah couldn't help but be drawn in by the beauty of the chanting and the rhythmic flow of the service. There was no flashy presentation, no emotional appeals—just a deep, steady reverence for something beyond the ordinary.

For the first time, Sarah felt that there was something in this world that couldn't be explained by science. The beauty and mystery of the liturgy spoke to a part of her that had long been neglected—the part that yearned for meaning, for connection with something greater than herself.

After the service, Sarah met with Peter and Father John, the parish priest. She had a million questions, and Father John patiently answered them. She asked about the liturgy, the icons, the prayers—everything she had witnessed that day. But what intrigued her most was the Orthodox understanding of the relationship between faith and reason.

"In Orthodoxy," Father John explained, "we believe that faith and reason complement each other. God gave us minds to explore and understand the world He created. Science is a way to discover the order and beauty of that creation. But faith helps us to see the deeper purpose behind it. It's not just about the mechanics of how the universe works—it's about understanding our place in it and our relationship with God."

Sarah was fascinated by the idea that faith didn't have to contradict science. For so long, she had assumed that religion demanded a rejection of rational thought. But here was a tradition that saw faith as something that worked alongside reason, not against it. The more she learned, the more she realized that Orthodoxy offered a way of seeing the world that she had never encountered before—a way that embraced both the mind and the soul.

Over the following months, Sarah found herself drawn more deeply into the life of the Orthodox Church. She continued to attend liturgies and began reading the works of the Church Fathers, who spoke of creation as a reflection of God's wisdom. Saints like St. Basil the Great and St. Gregory of Nyssa wrote about the natural world in ways that resonated with her as a scientist. They didn't see creation as something separate from God, but as a means of knowing Him more fully.

One night, after a particularly moving liturgy, Sarah had a conversation with Father John about her struggles to reconcile her scientific worldview with the concept of God. She confessed that, while she was deeply moved by the beauty of the liturgy and the teachings of the Church, she still found it difficult to make the leap from reason to faith.

Father John nodded understandingly. "Sarah, faith isn't about rejecting reason—it's about allowing reason to be fulfilled in something greater. You've spent your life exploring the wonders of creation through science, and that's a good thing. But science can only take us so far. It tells us *how* things work, but it doesn't tell us *why*. Faith gives us the deeper answers to those questions—answers that go beyond what we can observe."

Sarah pondered his words. It was true that science had given her a way to understand the mechanics of the world, but it hadn't answered the deeper questions she had been grappling with: Why are we here? What is the purpose of life? Is there something beyond the physical world? For the first time, Sarah began to realize that her search for meaning had been incomplete without faith.

As time went on, Sarah found herself drawn more deeply into the sacramental life of the Church. The Orthodox emphasis on *theosis*—the process of becoming united with God through His grace—resonated with her in a profound way. It wasn't about abandoning her scientific pursuits; it was about seeing them in a new light. The more she understood about the natural world, the more it pointed her toward the Creator.

Eventually, Sarah made the decision to be baptized into the Western Orthodox Church. It was a decision that felt both surprising and inevitable, as if all her years of scientific inquiry had been leading her to this moment. On the day of her baptism, as she stood before the altar, surrounded by candles and icons, Sarah felt a deep sense of peace. This was the peace she had been searching for all her life—not the fleeting satisfaction of intellectual discovery, but the lasting peace that came from knowing God.

As Father John poured the water over her head and anointed her with holy oil, Sarah felt as if a weight had been lifted from her shoulders. She no longer had to choose between science and faith. In Orthodoxy, she had found a tradition that embraced both, allowing her to explore the mysteries of the universe while also embracing the mystery of God.

In the months that followed, Sarah's life began to change in subtle but profound ways. Her work as a scientist took on new meaning, as she saw her research as a way to understand and glorify the Creator. Her prayers became more focused, and she found joy in the daily rhythms of the Orthodox spiritual life. She no longer felt the tension between reason and faith. Instead, she saw them as two sides of the same coin—both leading her deeper into the truth of God's creation.

Sarah's journey from skepticism to faith had not been easy, but it had been transformative. She had discovered that science and faith were not enemies, but partners in the search for truth. And in Orthodoxy, she had found the fullness of that truth—a truth that went beyond the limits of human reason and embraced the mystery of God.

The Spiritual Wanderer

Miguel had always been a seeker. Raised in a nominally Catholic family, he had gone through the motions of faith as a child—attending Mass, saying prayers before meals, and participating in religious holidays—but religion had never been central to his life. As he grew older, Miguel drifted away from the Church, drawn instead to spiritual paths that promised personal enlightenment and inner peace. By the time he entered college, he had fully embraced the identity of a "spiritual wanderer."

Miguel's bookshelf was filled with titles on Eastern meditation, New Age spirituality, mindfulness, and self-help. He dabbled in yoga, attended Buddhist retreats, and read about the mystical traditions of various cultures. For a while, these practices brought him a sense of peace, or at least the illusion of it. Yet, no matter how many techniques he tried, no matter how many spiritual books he read, there was an emptiness that lingered just beneath the surface. He was constantly searching for something deeper, something that would truly satisfy the longing in his heart.

Despite his best efforts, Miguel's spiritual life felt fragmented. Each new practice or philosophy seemed to offer a piece of the puzzle, but nothing ever seemed to fit together into a coherent whole. His days were filled with rituals and meditations, but his nights were haunted by a growing sense of restlessness and uncertainty. What was the point of all this spiritual seeking if it didn't lead him to something real?

During this period of uncertainty, Miguel reconnected with an old friend, Sarah, who had recently converted to Western Orthodoxy. They had known each other in high school, where they both shared an interest in philosophy and spiritual exploration. But while Miguel had drifted from Catholicism into a variety of spiritual paths, Sarah had been on a different journey—a journey that had led her to embrace the ancient Christian faith of Orthodoxy.

When they met for coffee one afternoon, Miguel was eager to share the latest spiritual retreat he had attended, a week-long meditation workshop that promised to unlock the secrets of inner peace. But as Sarah listened, she remained calm, responding with kindness but also with an inner peace that intrigued Miguel.

"What have you been up to?" Miguel asked, curious to hear about Sarah's life.

"I've been attending a Western Orthodox church," she replied. "It's been a transformative experience for me. I've found a deep sense of peace and connection with God that I never had before."

Miguel raised an eyebrow. "Orthodoxy? Isn't that... well, a bit traditional for someone like you? I always thought you were into exploring different spiritual paths."

Sarah smiled. "I was, for a long time. But eventually, I realized that all my searching wasn't leading me anywhere. I kept chasing after different practices and ideas, but none of it gave me what I was really looking for. It wasn't until I found Orthodoxy that I discovered the depth and fullness I had been searching for all along."

Intrigued but skeptical, Miguel asked her more about Orthodoxy. Sarah explained the ancient Christian tradition, the richness of the liturgy, the importance of the sacraments, and the concept of *theosis*—the process of becoming one with God through His grace. She spoke of how, in Orthodoxy, spirituality wasn't about discovering something within oneself, but about being transformed by the grace of God. It was a life of prayer, fasting, repentance, and community—a journey that led not to self-discovery but to union with Christ.

Miguel found himself intrigued by the idea of *theosis*. In all his years of spiritual searching, he had never encountered a tradition that spoke of transformation in such a profound way. Every spiritual path he had explored seemed focused on self-improvement, but here was a faith that spoke of surrendering oneself to God in order to be made new.

Still, he wasn't ready to dive in just yet. He had spent so many years exploring different spiritual traditions, and Orthodoxy seemed too rigid, too steeped in tradition and ritual for someone like him. Yet, something about Sarah's words stuck with him. There was a depth and wisdom in what she was saying that Miguel hadn't encountered in the New Age circles he frequented.

A few weeks later, Miguel found himself standing outside the Western Orthodox church that Sarah attended. He wasn't sure what had drawn him there—maybe it was curiosity, maybe it was the longing for something real, something that all his other spiritual pursuits hadn't been able to offer. As he stepped inside, he was immediately struck by the beauty and stillness of the space. The icons on the walls, the flickering candles, the faint scent of incense—it all created an atmosphere of deep reverence.

The liturgy began, and Miguel was captivated by the chanting, the prayers, and the sense of timelessness that filled the room. There was a solemnity to the service that felt sacred, unlike anything he had experienced before. This wasn't about self-improvement or enlightenment—it was about encountering the divine, about participating in something that had been passed down through centuries.

For the first time in years, Miguel felt a deep sense of peace, not the fleeting peace he had tried to cultivate through meditation or self-help techniques, but a peace that came from outside of himself. As he listened to the prayers and watched the faithful receive the Eucharist, he realized that this was what he had been searching for all along—a faith that wasn't about him, but about God.

After the service, Miguel stayed behind, quietly sitting in the pews, contemplating what he had just experienced. Father Gregory, the priest, noticed him and approached with a kind smile.

"Is this your first time attending an Orthodox service?" Father Gregory asked gently.

Miguel nodded. "Yeah, it's... different from anything I've experienced before. I've been searching for something deeper, but I've never quite found it. I've explored all kinds of spiritual paths, but nothing seems to stick. There's something about this... about what you're doing here... that feels real."

Father Gregory listened thoughtfully. "Many people come to Orthodoxy after years of searching. We live in a world that offers so many different spiritual options, but often, they're focused on the self—on finding something within, on self-improvement or enlightenment. Orthodoxy is different. It's not about discovering yourself. It's about surrendering yourself to God, allowing Him to transform you through His grace."

Miguel felt something stir inside him as he heard those words. Surrendering himself to God? It was a completely different way of thinking from everything he had been taught in the spiritual paths he had followed. But the idea of being transformed by something greater than himself was compelling. Maybe, just maybe, this was the answer he had been seeking all along.

Over the next few months, Miguel began attending the Orthodox liturgy regularly. He continued to read about the faith, immersing himself in the writings of the Church Fathers and learning more about the theology of *theosis*. He discovered that Orthodoxy wasn't about following rigid rules or rituals for their own sake. It was about entering into a relationship with the living God, a relationship that transformed every part of one's life.

The idea of *theosis*—of becoming one with God through His grace—became the heart of Miguel's spiritual journey. For so long, he had sought spiritual fulfillment through his own efforts, but now he realized that true transformation could only come through the grace of God. It wasn't about trying harder or mastering more techniques. It was about surrendering his will, his desires, and his very self to God, trusting that He would do the work of transformation.

Eventually, Miguel made the decision to be baptized into the Orthodox Church. His journey from spiritual wandering to Orthodoxy had been long and winding, filled with detours and dead ends, but he knew now that he had found his home. On the day of his baptism, standing before the altar, Miguel felt a deep sense of peace. This was not the peace of fleeting emotions or temporary spiritual highs—it was the peace that came from knowing that he was in the presence of God, and that God was at work in his life.

As the priest poured the water over him and anointed him with oil, Miguel felt the weight of years of searching and striving lift from his shoulders. He was no longer a wanderer, lost and searching for meaning in a thousand different spiritual practices. He had found the One who had been seeking him all along—the God who had created him, loved him, and now called him to a life of communion with Him.

In the months that followed, Miguel's life changed in ways he never expected. His prayers became deeper and more focused, no longer centered on himself but on God's will. He found joy in the simplicity of the Orthodox spiritual disciplines—prayer, fasting, confession, and the Eucharist. The faith that had once seemed so rigid and traditional now felt like a source of freedom, a path that led to true spiritual growth.

Miguel's journey from spiritual wandering to Orthodoxy wasn't about rejecting the truths he had found in other traditions—it was about finding the fullness of those truths in Christ. In Orthodoxy, he had discovered a faith that was both ancient and alive, a faith that called him to surrender his life to God in order to be transformed by His grace.

For Miguel, the journey was far from over. He knew that the process of *theosis*—of becoming one with God—was a lifelong path. But now, he walked that path with confidence, knowing that he was no longer wandering. He had found the way, the truth, and the life in Christ, and in Him, he had found the peace he had been searching for all along.

The Evangelical's Awakening

Rebecca had grown up in a fervent Evangelical home. Her parents were deeply committed Christians, and from a young age, Rebecca absorbed their devotion. Sundays were spent at church, where the sermons were fiery and passionate, always calling people to make a personal commitment to Jesus. She loved the vibrant energy of her faith community—there was a sense of immediacy to everything they did, from worship to prayer. Everyone was encouraged to build a personal relationship with Jesus, to accept Him into their hearts as their Savior, and to evangelize to others.

As a teenager, Rebecca was very active in her church. She sang in the worship band, led youth groups, and often prayed with others during altar calls. Evangelicalism had given her a deep, emotional connection to Jesus. She loved her faith and the community that came with it. Yet, as she grew older, she began to sense that something was missing. The constant focus on personal feelings and individual relationships with Jesus, though powerful, seemed to lack depth. Rebecca felt there was something more—a richness that her spiritual life was missing.

She began to ask questions about church history and the teachings of the early Church. Rebecca's pastors, while well-meaning, often brushed these questions aside, focusing instead on the necessity of a personal relationship with Christ and Bible study. But Rebecca couldn't shake the feeling that the faith she had grown up with was missing something ancient and foundational—something that could ground her deeper in the Gospel.

During her college years, Rebecca's desire to explore these deeper questions grew stronger. She read about the early Church Fathers and was struck by their profound devotion to Christ and the sacraments. She came across writings by St. Ignatius of Antioch, St. Justin Martyr, and St. Irenaeus, all of whom spoke of the Eucharist as the real presence of Christ, not merely as a symbolic remembrance. She was particularly struck by how they spoke of the Church as a living body—connected, unified, and sacramental. This understanding of the Church seemed so different from the fragmented denominations she had known all her life.

Curious and seeking answers, Rebecca decided to visit a Western Orthodox church. She had heard about Orthodoxy but had never given it much thought. To her, it seemed exotic, foreign, and perhaps a bit intimidating. Yet the more she read, the more she felt compelled to see for herself what this ancient Christian tradition was all about.

The first time Rebecca stepped into the Western Orthodox church, she felt like she had entered a different world. The quiet reverence, the flickering candles, the icons surrounding the sanctuary—it was all so different from the contemporary worship services she had grown up with. There were no electric guitars, no stage lights, no emotional altar calls. Instead, there was a profound stillness, a sense that she was standing in the presence of something ancient and holy.

As the liturgy began, Rebecca was taken aback by the beauty and formality of the service. The chanting of the priest, the incense rising to the heavens, the careful movements of the deacon—everything seemed to have a purpose. It wasn't about entertaining the congregation or evoking an emotional response. It was about worshipping God in spirit and truth, about participating in something much larger than herself.

During the Eucharist, Rebecca watched as the priest carefully prepared the bread and wine, speaking prayers that had been handed down through centuries. When the priest elevated the chalice and proclaimed, "The Body and Blood of Christ," Rebecca felt something stir deep within her. She had always believed that Communion was symbolic, but here was a church that believed in the real, tangible presence of Christ in the Eucharist.

After the service, Rebecca stayed in the pews, quietly reflecting on what she had just experienced. She felt overwhelmed, not by emotion, but by a sense of awe. There was a depth to the liturgy that resonated with her in a way she had never felt before. It wasn't about how she felt or what she was thinking—it was about encountering Christ in a way that transcended words and emotions.

Rebecca returned to the Western Orthodox church the following Sunday, and the Sunday after that. Each time, she found herself drawn deeper into the mystery of the liturgy. The prayers, the hymns, the icons—they all seemed to point to a reality that was much greater than her own personal experience. She began meeting with the priest,

Father Timothy, asking him questions about Orthodoxy, the sacraments, and church history.

"What's different about Orthodoxy?" Rebecca asked one day. "I've always been taught that it's all about a personal relationship with Jesus. But here, it feels like there's so much more."

Father Timothy smiled gently. "Orthodoxy teaches that our personal relationship with Jesus is essential, but it's only part of the picture. We are not just individuals in isolation. We are part of the body of Christ, the Church. Our relationship with Christ is lived out in communion with others, and in the sacraments, we encounter Christ in a very real way. The Eucharist, for example, is not just a symbol. It is the real presence of Christ, given to us for the life of the world."

Rebecca nodded thoughtfully. She had always believed in Jesus and loved Him deeply, but she began to realize that her faith had been missing the communal and sacramental aspects of the Christian life. It wasn't just about "me and Jesus." It was about being part of a living, breathing body—the Church—that had been united in Christ for two thousand years.

As she continued attending the Orthodox church, Rebecca's understanding of worship began to shift. She had always been taught that worship was about expressing her love and devotion to God, but in Orthodoxy, she learned that worship was about entering into the heavenly liturgy, joining with the angels and saints in glorifying God. It wasn't about creating a certain emotional experience—it was about participating in the eternal worship of God, both in heaven and on earth.

The idea of *theosis*—becoming one with God through His grace—also captivated Rebecca. In her Evangelical background, salvation had been framed primarily in terms of being saved from sin and going to heaven when she died. But in Orthodoxy, salvation was understood as a process of transformation, of becoming more and more like Christ. It wasn't just about avoiding hell or gaining entrance into heaven. It was about being made holy, being united with God in a relationship of love that began here and now.

After months of prayer, study, and reflection, Rebecca made the decision to be chrismated into the Western Orthodox Church. It was not a rejection of her Evangelical roots—she still valued the deep love for Christ that she had learned growing up. But she now saw that her faith journey had brought her to a place where that love could be deepened, enriched by the ancient wisdom and practices of the Orthodox Church.

On the day of her chrismation, Rebecca stood at the front of the church, surrounded by icons and candles. As Father Timothy anointed her with holy oil, she felt a profound sense of peace. This was not the emotional high she had often felt during altar calls or worship services in her Evangelical past. It was deeper than that—a quiet, steady sense that she had found her spiritual home.

As she received the Eucharist for the first time, Rebecca understood what the Church Fathers had meant when they spoke of the real presence of Christ in the sacrament. It was not just a symbol—it was a mystery, a sacred encounter with the risen Christ. She had finally found the depth and richness she had been searching for all along.

In the months that followed, Rebecca's faith grew in ways she had never imagined. The prayers of the Orthodox Church, the icons, the daily rhythm of the liturgical calendar—all of it drew her deeper into the mystery of Christ. She no longer felt the pressure to "feel" a certain way in worship. Instead, she rested in the knowledge that she was participating in something much greater than herself—the eternal worship of God.

Rebecca's journey from Evangelical Christianity to Orthodoxy was not about rejecting the love for Jesus she had known all her life. It was about discovering the fullness of that love, expressed not only in a personal relationship but in communion with the Church, in the sacraments, and in the transformative grace of God. She had awakened to a faith that was deeper, richer, and more ancient than she had ever imagined—a faith that would continue to shape her life for years to come.

The Secular Humanist's

Search

Daniel had always prided himself on his rational approach to life. Raised in a family that valued education, critical thinking, and ethics, Daniel became a firm believer in secular humanism during his university years. To him, the idea of relying on faith for guidance or meaning was unnecessary. The world, with its complexities and challenges, could be navigated through human intellect and empathy alone. Religion, Daniel believed, was simply a crutch for those too afraid to confront the uncertainties of life.

Secular humanism offered Daniel a clear, ethical framework. He found comfort in the belief that human beings had the power to shape their own destinies through reason, moral philosophy, and collective effort. He believed in the inherent goodness of people and that society could progress towards a better, more just future if only they relied on these principles. He devoted much of his time to causes related to social justice, human rights, and environmental protection, believing that these efforts would help make the world a better place.

Despite his sense of purpose, Daniel couldn't shake a feeling of dissatisfaction that had quietly grown over the years. His focus on making the world a better place didn't seem to fill a deeper emptiness that he was becoming increasingly aware of. When he went to bed at night, after a long day of work and activism, there was a gnawing sense that something was missing. He told himself that it was just the human condition—that he was simply grappling with existential questions that everyone faced. But even his reasoning failed to bring him the peace he so desperately sought.

His wife, Laura, had always been more spiritually inclined. Though she respected his beliefs, she had grown up in a Western Orthodox family and often encouraged Daniel to explore faith with an open mind. She never pressured him but spoke occasionally about how her faith gave her a sense of peace and stability, especially in difficult times. Daniel listened but was always careful to deflect the conversation, not wanting to delve into something that he considered irrational.

However, after a particularly difficult year—a combination of personal loss, professional stress, and a growing sense of disillusionment with the political and social movements he once believed would bring about lasting change—Daniel began to question everything. The world, as much as he wanted to believe otherwise, didn't seem to be getting any better. Even the causes he had dedicated his life to seemed mired in endless conflict, division, and inefficacy. For the first time, Daniel found himself wondering whether there was something more, something he hadn't considered.

It was during this time of internal turmoil that Laura invited him to attend a Western Orthodox liturgy. Daniel hesitated, but seeing how much peace her faith seemed to bring her, he agreed. At the very least, he told himself, it would be an interesting cultural experience.

The moment Daniel stepped into the small, ancient church, he felt a sense of reverence that was entirely foreign to him. The beauty of the icons, the flickering candles, and the gentle scent of incense all contributed to an atmosphere of mystery and sacredness. It was a stark contrast to the world he had known—one filled with noise, conflict, and intellectual debates. Here, there was a stillness, a peace that seemed to transcend time.

As the liturgy began, Daniel was struck by the chanting of the priests and the congregation. The words were ancient, rooted in a tradition that stretched back thousands of years. Despite his secular upbringing, he felt something stir within him, something he couldn't quite explain. There was a deep sense of awe, as if he were in the presence of something far greater than himself. For the first time in years, he didn't feel the need to explain or rationalize everything. He simply let himself experience the moment.

The liturgy was unlike anything Daniel had ever witnessed. It was slow, deliberate, and full of symbolism. There were no flashy sermons or impassioned appeals to emotion—just quiet, reverent prayer. As he observed the congregation, he noticed something remarkable: these people weren't here out of obligation or habit. They were here because they believed they were in the presence of God, and that belief was reflected in every movement, every word, every gesture.

After the service, Daniel and Laura stayed for a while, sitting quietly in the pews. Daniel couldn't deny the impact the experience had on him. He felt an overwhelming sense of peace, unlike anything he had felt in his secular pursuits. But at the same time, it raised more questions than answers.

Later that evening, as they sat together at home, Daniel asked Laura about what he had experienced. "Why do you come to church?" he asked. "What is it that you find here that you can't find anywhere else?"

Laura smiled gently. "For me, it's not about finding something outside of myself. It's about being in the presence of God, the Creator of everything, and recognizing that He is greater than my thoughts, my plans, or even my understanding. Orthodoxy teaches that we are called to *theosis*—becoming one with God, allowing His grace to transform us. It's not about fixing the world with human effort alone. It's about surrendering to God's will and letting Him change us from the inside out."

Daniel was intrigued. The idea of *theosis*—becoming one with God—was completely foreign to his secular humanist worldview, but it struck a chord with the questions he had been grappling with. For so long, he had relied on human intellect and effort to make sense of the world, but perhaps there was something deeper, something beyond reason that could offer true transformation.

Over the next few weeks, Daniel continued attending liturgy with Laura, each time finding himself more drawn to the stillness and reverence of the Orthodox Church. He began to read more about the faith, particularly the writings of the early Church Fathers. He was struck by how Orthodoxy didn't dismiss reason or intellect, but rather saw them as part of a larger journey toward communion with God. In Orthodoxy, faith and reason weren't at odds—they were complementary, each leading toward a deeper understanding of truth.

One day, after several months of attending services and studying the faith, Daniel met with Father Gregory, the priest of the church. He was full of questions—about the nature of God, the role of prayer, and the Orthodox understanding of salvation. Father Gregory listened patiently and answered Daniel's questions with wisdom and humility.

"What I've learned in my secular life," Daniel began, "is that reason can take us so far, but it doesn't seem to answer the deeper questions. How can we know that there's anything beyond this life? Beyond what we can see and touch?"

Father Gregory smiled. "That's a question many people ask, especially those who come from a background like yours. In Orthodoxy, we don't just know God through intellect or reason. We experience Him. The Church teaches that God is not distant or unknowable—He revealed Himself to us through Jesus Christ. And through the sacraments, through prayer, through the liturgy, we come into communion with Him. It's not about having all the answers. It's about being open to His grace, allowing Him to reveal Himself to you in ways beyond what you can measure or prove."

Daniel nodded slowly, understanding that faith wasn't about abandoning reason—it was about embracing something greater than reason could fully comprehend. He had spent so long trying to solve the world's problems with human effort, but now he realized that true transformation had to begin with something deeper—something spiritual.

After several months of continued reflection and prayer, Daniel made the decision to be baptized into the Western Orthodox Church. His journey had been long and filled with doubts, but he knew that this was where he belonged. The faith he had once dismissed as irrational had become the source of the peace he had long sought.

On the day of his baptism, standing in the quiet of the church, holding a lit candle, Daniel felt a deep sense of peace. He had come to realize that the emptiness he had felt for so long couldn't be filled by human effort or reason alone. It could only be filled by God—by surrendering to His love and grace, and by allowing Him to transform his heart.

As the priest anointed him with oil, Daniel felt a profound sense of belonging. He had spent so much of his life searching for meaning, but now, in the Orthodox Church, he had found not just answers, but a relationship with the living God. It was a relationship that went beyond intellect, beyond human effort—a relationship rooted in love, grace, and transformation.

In the months that followed, Daniel's life began to change in subtle but profound ways. He continued his work in social justice and human rights, but now with a renewed sense of purpose. He no longer believed that the world could be fixed by human hands alone—he knew that true change came from God. And as he grew in his faith, as he embraced the sacramental life of the Church, he found the peace that had eluded him for so long.

Daniel's journey from secular humanism to Orthodoxy was not about abandoning reason, but about finding the balance between reason and faith. He had learned that human intellect, while powerful, could only take him so far. In Orthodoxy, he had discovered the fullness of truth—the truth that God is real, that He loves us, and that through His grace, we can be transformed. And in that transformation, Daniel had found the peace he had longed for.

The Former Catholic's Homecoming

Katie's Journey to Orthodoxy:
Finding the Ancient Faith in a Changing World

A Growing Discontent: Modernism Creeping into the Roman Catholic Church

Katie had spent her entire life within the **Roman Catholic Church**—baptized as an infant, raised in a devout household, and deeply committed to the teachings and practices of the Church. For decades, Catholicism was her foundation, giving her a strong sense of belonging, structure, and spiritual purpose. Yet in recent years, Katie began to feel unsettled. **Changes within the Church of Rome**—new teachings, shifts in liturgical practices, and what she saw as an **embrace of modern cultural trends**—

left her feeling disconnected from the faith she once held so firmly.

Katie's discomfort grew as she heard **statements from Pope Francis** that seemed to suggest a broader acceptance of beliefs and practices outside traditional Catholic teachings. Phrases such as **"Who am I to judge?"** and the increasing focus on **dialogue with non-Christian religions** troubled her. While she valued compassion and open-mindedness, Katie began to feel that the Church was **losing its anchor**, allowing modernism to dilute the teachings of Christ. She noticed changes in the **liturgy**, the **moral teachings**, and even in **priestly formation**, and she struggled with the creeping sense that the Church she loved was becoming **more accommodating to the world than faithful to God.**

What Katie found particularly disheartening was the suggestion that **salvation could be found even outside of explicit faith in Christ**. Statements implying that **atheists and adherents of other religions could attain salvation** without participation in the sacraments struck a deep chord of conflict within her. **"If salvation can be found outside the Church,"** she wondered, **"then what is the point of the sacraments, of prayer, of the Cross itself?"**

Her frustration deepened when the Church began emphasizing **diversity and inclusiveness** in ways that seemed to **contradict centuries of doctrinal consistency**. At the same time, Katie saw a growing acceptance of **moral relativism**, with the Church softening its stance on issues she believed were central to the faith. She felt that **truth was being sacrificed for the sake of cultural**

relevance. This growing disillusionment left her searching for something deeper, more rooted, and unchanging.

A Chance Encounter with Orthodoxy

Amid her spiritual turmoil, Katie's life took a surprising turn. A close friend, Maria, who was **Orthodox**, invited her to attend a **Divine Liturgy** at a small parish nearby. Katie had heard of Orthodoxy but knew very little about it. Out of curiosity—and perhaps desperation—she accepted the invitation.

From the moment she entered the church, Katie felt transported to another world. The rich scent of **incense**, the sound of **chanting**, and the sight of **icons illuminating the walls** evoked a sense of ancient beauty and reverence. There were no screens, no attempts to modernize or accommodate trends. The liturgy felt **timeless**, as if it belonged to another era—one untouched by the shifting sands of contemporary culture.

As Katie stood quietly, listening to the prayers in the Divine Liturgy, she felt something stir within her: **a sense of awe and reverence she hadn't felt in years**. It was as though she had rediscovered a treasure she didn't know she was missing.

The Struggle with Theological Differences: Theosis and Synergy

Yet, as compelling as her experience of the liturgy was, **theology remained a significant hurdle**. Orthodox teachings on **theosis**—the process of becoming one with God through His grace—challenged her deeply. Katie had always believed in **sanctification**, but the Orthodox understanding of **sharing in God's divine nature** was difficult to grasp. **"Aren't we supposed to follow God, not become like Him?"** she asked Maria.

Maria explained that **theosis does not mean becoming God by essence**, but rather **being transformed by His grace** into His likeness. As **2 Peter 1:4** states, believers are invited to **become partakers of the divine nature**. It was not about self-exaltation but about **humble participation in God's life through prayer, fasting, and the sacraments**.

Katie also struggled with the concept of synergism—the idea that **salvation involves cooperation between God's grace and human effort**. In Roman Catholicism, salvation was primarily seen as a work of God through the sacraments, and while personal effort was emphasized, **Orthodoxy's focus on synergy seemed overwhelming**. It required her to rethink her understanding of **faith as both gift and responsibility**—an ongoing relationship with God that required her active participation.

Letting Go of Purgatory: A Difficult Step

Another theological struggle was **Orthodoxy's rejection of purgatory**. Katie had long found comfort in the idea that souls could undergo **purification after death** to enter heaven fully prepared. **The Council of Florence (1439)** and **the Council of Trent (1545-1563)** had cemented the doctrine of purgatory as a place where the faithful, though saved, still needed cleansing from **temporal punishment** for sin. This belief was deeply embedded in Katie's spirituality. **Prayers for the dead, indulgences, and Masses offered for souls in purgatory** were familiar practices she had relied on for years.

In Orthodoxy, she learned, there is no doctrine of purgatory. The focus is on **preparing the soul now, in this life**, through **repentance and participation in the sacraments**. Though Orthodoxy encourages **prayers for the departed**, it leaves the state of the soul after death to **God's mercy**. At first, this unsettled Katie. **"What happens to those who aren't perfect when they die?"** she asked. The priest explained that **Orthodoxy places its trust in God's mercy and encourages the living to pray fervently for the dead, without defining a specific place or process of postmortem purification.**

The Challenge of Identity: Letting Go and Moving Forward

Perhaps the hardest part of Katie's journey was **letting go of her Catholic identity.** She had spent a lifetime defending the Church's teachings, celebrating its sacraments, and relying on its structure for spiritual guidance. **Becoming Orthodox felt like betraying the faith that had shaped her.**

Maria gently reminded Katie that **Orthodoxy does not condemn other Christian traditions** but recognizes that **God can work within many contexts.** However, the fullness of truth, Orthodoxy teaches, lies within the **Apostolic faith** preserved by the Church from the beginning. **"God has been with you every step of your journey,"** Maria said. **"Now He's calling you deeper."**

Katie came to understand that **conversion to Orthodoxy was not a rejection of her past** but a **fulfillment of her faith journey.** It was not about discarding the good she had experienced but about **entering into the fullness of what God had prepared for her.**

Receiving the Sacraments: A New Beginning

After months of attending liturgies, participating in **catechism classes,** and wrestling with her doubts, Katie made the decision to **become Orthodox**. On the day of her **chrismation,** she stood before the priest, holding an icon of **Christ the Pantocrator**. As the priest anointed her with **holy chrism,** Katie felt a profound sense of peace. **"This is where God has been leading me all along,"** she thought.

Receiving the **Eucharist** for the first time as an Orthodox Christian was a moment of deep spiritual significance. She realized that in Orthodoxy, the Eucharist was not just a sacrament but **a mystical union with Christ,** a foretaste of eternal life. **Her past faith had not been abandoned but fulfilled**—transformed by the ancient practices of the Church.

Conclusion: Embracing the Ancient Path of Theosis

Katie's journey to Orthodoxy was not without struggle. It required her to **let go of deeply held beliefs** about **purgatory, papal authority, and salvation,** while embracing new teachings on **theosis, synergy, and repentance**. Yet, through prayer, humility, and God's grace, she discovered that the **ancient faith of Orthodoxy** offered a stability and fullness that she had long sought.

Her discontent with the **modernist trends** within Roman Catholicism was not the end of her faith journey but the beginning of a new chapter—one rooted in the

unchanging truth of the Apostolic faith. Through
Orthodoxy, Katie found what she had been searching for: **a
path of love, prayer, and sacramental life leading
toward union with God.**

From Evangelical Zeal to Orthodox Home

Jacob had always been a man of deep faith. Raised in a fervent Evangelical household, he learned early on that a personal relationship with Jesus was the cornerstone of salvation. From his teenage years onward, Jacob was a leader in his church youth groups, memorizing scripture and sharing his faith with passion. His zeal was evident, and his commitment to Christ was sincere. Yet, over time, Jacob began to feel a growing sense of unrest.

As a young man, Jacob had witnessed the division and fragmentation within Evangelical Christianity. The constant denominational splits, varying interpretations of scripture, and endless debates over theological points troubled him deeply. How could the Gospel of Christ, which he believed to be simple and clear, lead to so much confusion and division?

Seeking a more unified Christian experience, Jacob found his way to the Roman Catholic Church. The Catholic claim of apostolic succession, its emphasis on tradition, and the sacraments initially seemed to offer the stability and continuity that Evangelicalism lacked. Jacob immersed himself in the teachings of the Church, finding solace in the reverence of the liturgy and the sacramental life. After years of discernment, Jacob became a Roman Catholic, believing he had finally discovered the fullness of the Christian faith.

For a time, his heart was at peace. The structured, ancient rhythm of the Catholic Church drew him in. He participated in the Mass with reverence and dedication, admiring the Church's history and its authority. But as the years passed, Jacob noticed subtle changes within the Church—changes that deeply disturbed him.

In homilies, Jacob heard less about sin, repentance, and the narrow path to salvation, and more about inclusivity, modernization, and adapting to cultural shifts. He began to feel that the Gospel message, as Jesus had

287

proclaimed it, was being softened. Teachings on moral absolutes seemed to blur, replaced by a focus on tolerance and dialogue with secular culture. The final blow came when Jacob was invited to Rome as a participant in the *Synod on Synodality*—an event he had hoped would restore the Church to its roots but which ultimately left him even more disillusioned.

Jacob had been chosen as one of the diocease representatives to attend the synod because of his previous involvement in various theological discussions. It was considered an honor, and he was eager to take part in what he thought would be an opportunity to help guide the Church back to the firm teachings of Christ. However, once in Rome, Jacob quickly realized that the synod was not focused on upholding the timeless truths of the Gospel but rather on exploring how the Church could further embrace modern cultural values.

In discussions, he heard bishops and clergy talking about "accompaniment" and "pastoral flexibility" in ways that troubled him. When he raised concerns about the importance of adhering to Christ's words, particularly about the narrow way to salvation, he was met with condescending smiles. He brought up passages like Matthew 7:13-14, where Jesus clearly says that the path to life is narrow and few find it. To his dismay, many at the synod seemed more interested in expanding the path, accommodating contemporary sensibilities rather than reaffirming the hard truths of the Gospel.

The final session of the synod was what broke Jacob's heart. It was a session on "dialogue" with the modern world, and one of the participants—a cardinal—openly suggested that the Church might need to "rethink" certain moral teachings to better align with the shifting values of society. Jacob could hardly believe what he was hearing. This was not the Church of the Apostles, not the Church of Christ who had warned against conforming to the world. He had entered the Catholic Church seeking stability and truth, but now it seemed to be drifting away from the Gospel message that had drawn him to it in the first place.

Deeply shaken, Jacob returned home from Rome in a spiritual crisis. The Church he had embraced as the keeper of apostolic truth was now, in his eyes, more focused on modernity than fidelity to the teachings of Christ. He no longer felt confident that the path the Church was pursuing was the narrow way that Jesus spoke about. The disillusionment was overwhelming.

Jacob found himself in a period of spiritual desolation, unsure where to turn. It was during this time of confusion that he came across a book about the early Church Fathers. He had always admired the writings of the saints, but in his searching, he came across an ancient tradition that he had never fully explored—Eastern Orthodoxy.

He had been vaguely aware of Orthodoxy before, but had never considered it seriously. Now, feeling adrift, Jacob decided to learn more. The more he read, the more intrigued he became. Unlike both Evangelicalism and modern Roman Catholicism, Orthodoxy had not changed with the times. The teachings of the Church Fathers, the reverence for tradition, and the commitment to preserving the Apostolic faith seemed to resonate deeply with what Jacob had been searching for all along.

Jacob decided to visit a Western Orthodox parish. What he found there was a liturgy that felt timeless, untouched by modern trends or cultural pressures. The priest spoke with clarity about sin, repentance, and the path to salvation. The Eucharist, Jacob realized, was not just a symbol or a religious ritual—it was the real presence of Christ, unchanged since the days of the Apostles.

After the service, Jacob met with Father Gregory, the parish priest. "Father," Jacob said, "I've been searching for the true Church for years. I've been an Evangelical and a Catholic, but both paths seem to have strayed from the narrow way that Christ calls us to. I thought the Catholic Church would remain faithful, but even there I've seen a departure from the truth. I don't know where to turn."

Father Gregory listened patiently. "Jacob, many who come to Orthodoxy have felt that same longing for truth. The Church is not called to conform to the world. We are called to be faithful to the teachings of Christ and the Apostles. The narrow way isn't easy, but it's the path that leads to life. Orthodoxy has never changed its message because the truth doesn't change. It's not about being rigid or uncompromising for the sake of tradition—it's about preserving the faith once delivered to the saints."

Jacob began attending the liturgy regularly, immersing himself in the writings of the Church Fathers and learning about the Orthodox understanding of salvation. What struck him most was the emphasis on *theosis*—the process of becoming united with God through His grace. This was the narrow way, not a path of compromise or adapting to modern cultural norms, but one of genuine transformation into the likeness of Christ.

After months of prayer and discernment, Jacob made the decision to be chrismated into the Western Orthodox Church. His journey had been long and winding, filled with many challenges and doubts, but he finally felt at home in a Church that had remained faithful to the Gospel and the Christian First Principles passed down from the Apostles.

As he stood at the altar during his chrismation, Jacob felt a deep peace wash over him. He had found the narrow way, the path that Christ had spoken of so long ago. It wasn't an easy path, but it was the only one that led to life. And for Jacob, it was the path that had led him home.

In Orthodoxy, Jacob had found what he had been searching for all his life: a faith that was unchanging, unwavering, and rooted in the truth of Christ. A faith that didn't bend to the pressures of modernity but stood firm in the teachings of the Apostles. The narrow way had led him through many trials, but in the end, it had led him to the fullness of the Christian faith.

From Self to Surrender

Mark had always known he was different. From the time he was a young boy growing up in a devout Roman Catholic family, he felt a sense of alienation from the teachings of his church, though he couldn't quite articulate why. He loved the Church—its sacraments, the rhythm of the liturgical year, and the mystery of its ancient prayers. But when he became a teenager, that sense of difference came into sharp focus: he realized he was attracted to other men.

For years, Mark struggled to reconcile this part of himself with the Church's teachings. The Church was clear in its doctrine about sexual morality, but the cultural voices surrounding him told a different story. The world offered acceptance, affirmation, and even pride in what he was beginning to identify as his true self. The tension between his faith and his sexuality created an internal conflict that only grew as Mark entered his twenties.

Seeking peace, Mark distanced himself from the Church. He threw himself into communities that celebrated his identity, searching for fulfillment in the freedom they promised. Yet, despite the acceptance he found in the world, there remained an unshakable emptiness inside him. No relationship, no amount of affirmation, could fill the spiritual void that haunted him. He longed for something more—a deep peace that the world simply couldn't offer.

One night, after yet another relationship ended in heartbreak, Mark found himself alone in his apartment, scrolling aimlessly through the internet. A video caught his attention. It was of a priest discussing the teachings of Jesus on the cross, particularly the command to deny oneself and follow Christ. Mark clicked on it, drawn by a vague curiosity.

The priest's words were simple but deeply convicting. He quoted Jesus from the Gospel of Matthew: *"If anyone would come after me, let him deny himself and take up his cross and follow me"* (Matthew 16:24). The priest explained that this wasn't merely a call to avoid sin—it was an invitation to a new way of living, one rooted in surrender to Christ. True freedom, he said, comes not from indulging our desires but from offering them to God and allowing Him to transform us. The priest went on to talk about the importance of purity—not just as an abstract moral rule, but as a lifestyle rooted in the denial of self for the sake of Christ.

Mark was struck by the words. He had always thought of purity as an impossible standard, something for saints and monks, not for ordinary people like him. But this idea of self-denial—of surrendering desires, not as a rejection of himself, but as an act of love for Christ—was new. It felt like a key that unlocked something deep within him.

That night, Mark opened his Bible for the first time in years. He read through the Gospels, focusing especially on the passages where Jesus spoke of self-denial, sacrifice, and following Him. He realized that he had spent years trying to avoid what the Gospel was actually calling him to do: to deny himself, not out of self-hatred, but out of love for Christ.

For the first time, Mark began to see that his desires did not define him. His identity was not rooted in his sexuality but in his relationship with God. He saw clearly that the emptiness he had been feeling all those years was a result of trying to fill his life with things that could never satisfy his deepest longings. What he needed was Christ, and the only way to truly find Him was by surrendering everything to Him.

Feeling both convicted and hopeful, Mark began attending Mass again, but he found that something still wasn't quite right. The Church that he returned to felt different from the one he had left. There was a growing emphasis on modern interpretations of morality, and the clarity of the Church's teachings on self-denial and purity seemed to be fading. The homilies often centered on self-acceptance and inclusivity, and while those messages were important, Mark felt that something deeper was being lost.

In his search for more, Mark came across an article about Western Orthodoxy. It described the Orthodox Church's unwavering commitment to the ancient teachings of the Apostles, including a clear call to purity and self-denial. The article spoke of the Orthodox understanding of *theosis*—the process of becoming more like God through His grace, a transformation that required not just belief, but a whole-life surrender to Christ. Mark was intrigued.

He decided to attend a Western Orthodox liturgy. The moment he stepped into the church, Mark was struck by the beauty and reverence of the service. There was a profound sense of mystery and holiness in the liturgy, something that seemed to connect him to the ancient faith in a way he hadn't experienced before. The chanting, the incense, the prayers—all of it felt like a portal to a deeper reality.

After the service, Mark approached Father Stephen, the parish priest, and shared a bit of his journey. He spoke of his struggle to reconcile his faith with his sexuality and his newfound understanding of self-denial. Father Stephen listened patiently, then responded with words that would change Mark's life.

"Mark," Father Stephen said, "Jesus doesn't ask us to deny ourselves because He wants to take something away from us. He asks us to deny ourselves because it's the only way to truly find ourselves in Him. When we let go of our desires, we make space for Christ to fill us with His grace. Purity isn't just about avoiding sin—it's about being whole, about being fully alive in Christ. It's about letting His love transform every part of us."

Mark felt a deep sense of peace wash over him. Father Stephen's words made sense. Purity wasn't an unattainable ideal—it was the result of a life fully surrendered to Christ. It wasn't about repressing who he was, but about allowing Christ to transform him into who he was meant to be.

Over the next several months, Mark continued attending the liturgy and meeting with Father Stephen. He began to embrace the Orthodox teachings on asceticism and spiritual struggle, learning that denying oneself wasn't just a one-time decision but a daily choice to follow Christ. He learned that purity wasn't just about controlling physical desires—it was about aligning his heart, mind, and soul with the will of God.

Through the sacraments, especially Confession and the Eucharist, Mark began to experience the grace of God in ways he never had before. He realized that his journey wasn't just about overcoming a particular sin, but about being transformed into the likeness of Christ. The more he embraced self-denial and purity as a lifestyle, the more freedom he found—not the freedom to indulge his desires, but the freedom to love and serve God with his whole heart.

Eventually, Mark made the decision to be chrismated into the Western Orthodox Church. On the day of his chrismation, as Father Stephen anointed him with holy oil, Mark felt an overwhelming sense of joy and peace. He had spent so many years searching for fulfillment in the world, but now he understood that true fulfillment could only come through Christ—through the denial of self and the embrace of purity as a way of life.

Mark's journey was not easy, and he knew that the struggle for purity and holiness would continue for the rest of his life. But now, he had found the path—the narrow way that Jesus had spoken of. It was a path of self-denial, not for the sake of rejection, but for the sake of love—a love that called him to something higher, something greater than the world could offer.

In Orthodoxy, Mark had found the fullness of the faith, a faith that called him not to affirm his desires, but to offer them to Christ, trusting in His transformative power. By embracing purity as a lifestyle, Mark had discovered a peace that surpassed all understanding—a peace that could only come from walking in the footsteps of Christ.

The Journey of Ibrahim: From Islam to Western Orthodoxy

Ibrahim had always been a man of deep faith. Raised in a devout Muslim family, his days were structured around the call to prayer, the recitation of the Qur'an, and the five pillars of Islam. His father, a respected leader in their local mosque, taught him the importance of daily prayer, submission to Allah, and living a moral life according to Islamic principles. From a young age, Ibrahim took these teachings to heart. Faith was not just a part of his life—it *was* his life.

By the time Ibrahim reached his early twenties, however, he began to experience a quiet discontent. He had always found comfort in the discipline of prayer and the structure of Islam, but questions about the nature of God's love, the concept of salvation, and the identity of Jesus (Isa in Islam) began to weigh on him. Islam revered Jesus as a prophet, but Ibrahim couldn't shake the curiosity about the Christian claim that Jesus was more than just a prophet— that He was the Son of God.

During his university years, Ibrahim met Alex, a fellow student who had converted to Western Orthodoxy. They became fast friends, and over time, their conversations drifted toward theology. Alex spoke of the Incarnation—God becoming man—and the idea of *theosis*, which meant becoming one with God through His grace. This concept fascinated Ibrahim. He had never heard anything like it. The idea that God's desire was not only to guide humanity through His law but to unite Himself with humanity struck him as both strange and profound.

One afternoon, Alex invited Ibrahim to attend a Western Orthodox liturgy. Ibrahim hesitated, unsure of what to expect, but his curiosity got the better of him. The moment he entered the small church, he was enveloped by an atmosphere of reverence and stillness. The chanting of the liturgy, the burning incense, and the flickering candles brought a sense of peace that reminded Ibrahim of the structured, contemplative environment he had grown up with in Islam.

What struck Ibrahim most during the liturgy, however, was the prayer. The Orthodox Christians around him prayed not in a hurried or detached manner but with deep reverence, as if they truly believed they were standing in the presence of God. It wasn't unlike the way he had

299

learned to pray as a Muslim—with complete focus, submission, and dedication. The prayers of the Orthodox Church seemed to be woven into the fabric of daily life, much like the five daily prayers of Islam. This struck a familiar chord in Ibrahim, as he valued the discipline of regular, structured prayer.

After the service, Ibrahim approached Father Dimitri, the parish priest. He was full of questions, especially about the prayers and the Orthodox concept of *theosis*. "I've always prayed five times a day," Ibrahim said. "It's been part of my life since childhood. But the prayers here... they seem different. What do they mean, and what is this idea of becoming like God?"

Father Dimitri smiled warmly. "In Orthodoxy, we believe that prayer is not just a duty or an obligation, but a means of communion with God. Our daily prayers— whether in the liturgy or in private—are part of our relationship with God. Through prayer, we open ourselves to His grace, allowing Him to transform us from within. We call this process *theosis*—becoming one with God through His grace. It's not that we become God in His essence, but we participate in His divine life, becoming more like Him in holiness, love, and purity."

Ibrahim pondered this for a moment. In Islam, the focus of prayer was submission—bowing before Allah in obedience. Yet here, prayer seemed to go even deeper. It wasn't just submission but a kind of communion, an intimate relationship with God. The idea that God desired such closeness with humanity—that He became man in the person of Jesus Christ to unite Himself with us—was a profound and beautiful thought. Ibrahim was intrigued.

Over the next several weeks, Ibrahim began attending Orthodox services more regularly. He was particularly drawn to the rhythm of the daily prayers. He found the structure and discipline of Orthodoxy familiar, much like the prayer life he had grown up with in Islam. The Orthodox Church had morning and evening prayers, prayers before meals, and prayers for every part of life. There was a deep sense of continuity between his Muslim background and this Christian tradition—both emphasized the importance of regular, heartfelt prayer. But Orthodoxy offered something more: the idea that through prayer, one could participate in God's grace and grow in holiness.

Ibrahim also continued to ask Father Dimitri about *theosis*, as this concept resonated deeply with him. "Tell me more about how we become like God," he asked one evening.

Father Dimitri explained, "Theosis is the ultimate purpose of human life. In Orthodoxy, we believe that God became man in Jesus Christ so that we could share in His divine life. Through the Incarnation, God entered our humanity, so that we could be healed, transformed, and made whole. As we grow in holiness, through prayer, the sacraments, and the grace of God, we become more and more like Christ. Theosis is a lifelong journey of growing in the likeness of God, allowing His love to purify our hearts and our desires."

This idea of transformation struck Ibrahim deeply. In Islam, God was seen as distant and majestic, to be obeyed and revered. But here, in Orthodoxy, God was not distant—He was close, intimately involved in the lives of His people, desiring not just their submission but their transformation. Ibrahim began to realize that the restlessness he had felt for years was not just a longing for answers, but a longing for this deep communion with God.

One night, after months of prayer, study, and reflection, Ibrahim made a decision. He knelt in his room and whispered a simple prayer: "Lord Jesus Christ, if You truly are the Son of God, help me to follow You. Show me the way." In that moment, Ibrahim felt a deep sense of peace wash over him. It was as if the questions and doubts that had plagued him for so long had been answered—not intellectually, but in his heart. He knew that Jesus was the answer he had been searching for.

Shortly after, Ibrahim spoke to Father Dimitri about his desire to become an Orthodox Christian. The priest welcomed him warmly, and together they began the process of catechesis, where Ibrahim learned more about the faith, the sacraments, and the role of the Church. He found the teachings of Orthodoxy to be both challenging and liberating—challenging in their call to deny oneself and take up the cross, and liberating in the promise of transformation through God's grace.

The day of Ibrahim's baptism was one of profound joy. He stood before the altar, surrounded by the icons of Christ and the saints, ready to enter into the waters of new life. As Father Dimitri poured the water over him and anointed him with holy oil, Ibrahim felt a deep sense of belonging, as if he had finally come home. He was given a new name—Michael—after St. Michael the Archangel, a name that symbolized his new life in Christ and his spiritual battle for holiness.

As Michael, Ibrahim continued to embrace the Orthodox way of life. The discipline of daily prayer, which had been so central to his life as a Muslim, now took on new meaning. Each prayer was a moment of communion with God, a step on the path of *theosis*, the journey of becoming more like Christ. The sacraments, especially the Eucharist, became for him the source of divine grace, nourishing him as he walked the narrow way of salvation.

Michael's journey from Islam to Western Orthodoxy was not just a change in religious identity—it was a transformation of the heart. In Orthodoxy, he found the fulfillment of his longing for communion with God, a faith that called him to deny himself not out of duty, but out of love. Through prayer, the sacraments, and the grace of God, he had discovered the path of *theosis*—the journey of becoming one with God.

For Michael, Orthodoxy was not a rejection of his past but the fulfillment of it. The daily prayers, the structured rhythm of life, and the call to holiness all resonated with the deepest parts of his soul. He had found in Christ what he had been searching for all along—true communion with the living God. And in that communion, he found peace, transformation, and the promise of eternal life.

Author's Conversion Story

The Beginning: Faith in the Evangelical Tradition

My faith journey began in the **Evangelical Protestant tradition**, where I embraced a **personal relationship with Jesus** as the heart of Christianity. Growing up, I was deeply influenced by the **discipline of scripture reading, prayer, and personal conversion**, finding great comfort in the **worship and fellowship** of my Evangelical community. However, as I matured in my faith, I began to **sense that something was missing**. Despite the fervor and sincerity of the faith I practiced, I found myself longing for something with **greater depth, history, and continuity**—something connected to the early Church established by Christ and His Apostles.

As I immersed myself in the study of **scripture** and the teachings of the **Apostolic Church**, I found myself questioning the Evangelical concept of **sola scriptura**—the belief that **scripture alone** is the sole authority for faith and practice. It became increasingly clear to me that the earliest Christians did not rely solely on written texts; their faith was also nurtured by **sacraments, oral tradition, and Apostolic teaching**. This realization created a hunger within me for **deeper truths**—truths that could only be found in a **Church that had maintained the faith of the Apostles throughout the centuries**.

Considering Roman Catholicism: A Disillusioning Encounter with Modernism

As I sought a deeper connection with **historic Christianity**, I naturally looked to the **Roman Catholic Church**. With its claims of **Apostolic succession, ancient liturgical tradition**, and visible global presence, it seemed like the perfect place to find the spiritual stability I desired. However, as I explored the Roman Church, I began to notice troubling signs. Instead of preserving its ancient roots, the Catholic Church seemed to be **adapting to modern cultural trends**—compromising key elements of faith for the sake of relevance.

The **traditional aspects of the Church's liturgy** were being **marginalized or abandoned**, while **conservative priests and bishops**—those striving to uphold long-standing Church teachings—were **silenced or disciplined**. At the same time, **heretical clergy promoting progressive ideologies** were not only tolerated but often **promoted to leadership positions**.

I was particularly unsettled by **statements from Pope Francis**, suggesting that even **atheists and adherents of other religions** could achieve salvation outside the visible Church. This left me asking: **If salvation can be attained without Christ, what is the purpose of the sacraments and the Church itself?** What I had hoped would be **an anchor of stability** was, in fact, **drifting toward modernism**, further complicating my spiritual search.

A New Hope in the Old Catholic Church

Disillusioned with modern developments in the Roman Church, I turned to the **Old Catholic Church**. Founded in response to **the First Vatican Council's declaration of papal infallibility in 1870**, the Old Catholic movement seemed to offer a **path back to the authentic teachings of the early Church**. The **Declaration of Utrecht (1889)** immediately resonated with me. Its first article affirmed the teachings of the **first seven Ecumenical Councils**, rejected the **innovations of papal infallibility**, and upheld the importance of **sacramental life and Apostolic tradition**.

For someone like me—a **traditionally minded believer**—the Old Catholic Church seemed to be the perfect fit. It offered **the richness of the sacraments** without the **doctrinal excesses of Rome**. I embraced my calling within this tradition, **ordained as a priest** and eventually **consecrated as a bishop**. I poured myself into the **work of ministry,** shepherding the faithful and **administering the sacraments** with joy.

Disillusionment: Criticism and Assumptions About the Old Catholic Church

However, even within the Old Catholic Church, **disillusionment soon set in**. A major challenge I faced was the **near-constant criticism from other Christians**, who assumed that **our church was just as theologically liberal** as other Old Catholic jurisdictions. Many Old Catholic groups had embraced **progressive ideologies**—including **same-sex blessings, gender-fluid ordinations, and liturgical experimentation**—leading many to associate the entire Old Catholic movement with these practices.

While **our jurisdiction maintained a more traditional approach,** I often found myself **defending our teachings and practices** from those who accused us of abandoning the faith. The **misconceptions and criticisms** became exhausting. **How could I convince others that not all Old Catholic jurisdictions had compromised their theology?** It was frustrating to be **associated with theological positions** that contradicted **my own deeply held beliefs** and **the founding principles** of the Old Catholic Church.

Finding the Fullness of the Faith in Western Orthodoxy

As these frustrations grew, I began to explore **Orthodox Christianity**. What I found in Orthodoxy was **the stability and coherence** I had been seeking throughout my entire spiritual journey. Orthodoxy had preserved the **teachings of the Apostles without change for over two millennia**. It was neither **reactionary like Old Catholicism** nor **compromised like modern Roman Catholicism**. It offered a complete and unbroken connection to the **ancient faith**—a faith that was deeply sacramental, theologically rich, and spiritually transformative.

I was particularly drawn to **Western Orthodoxy**, which preserves the **Western liturgical heritage**—including the **Gregorian rite**—while remaining faithful to **Orthodox theology**. Here, I found **the best of both worlds**: the liturgical beauty of the Western tradition and the theological integrity of the ancient, **Apostolic faith**.

Theosis and Synergism: A New Understanding of Salvation

One of the most profound discoveries in Orthodoxy was the concept of **theosis**—the process of **becoming one with God through His uncreated grace**. Unlike the transactional view of salvation I had encountered in other traditions, Orthodoxy teaches that salvation is about **participating in the divine life**, allowing God's grace to **transform us from within**.

I also embraced **synergism**, the Orthodox understanding that **salvation requires cooperation between God's grace and human effort**. **St. Paul's words in Philippians 2:12-13** now resonated in a new way: "Work out your own salvation with fear and trembling, for it is God who works in you, both to will and to work for His good pleasure." Orthodoxy's view of salvation is neither passive nor self-reliant; it is a **dynamic relationship between divine grace and human response.**

Coming Home: Embracing Western Orthodoxy

After much prayer, study, and reflection, I knew that **Western Orthodoxy** was the spiritual home I had been seeking. I was **received into the Orthodox Church through chrismation**, marking the culmination of my long and difficult journey. Standing before the altar and receiving the **Eucharist** as an Orthodox Christian for the first time, I knew I had found the **fullness of the faith**—a faith that had remained **unchanged, stable, and complete.**

Serving as a Bishop in Western Orthodoxy

Today, I serve as a **bishop within The Holy Orthodox Catholic and Apostolic Church of America**. In this role, I have the privilege of **shepherding others along the path to theosis**, helping them discover the beauty and stability of **the Apostolic faith**. Western Orthodoxy offers a way for believers to **connect with the ancient Church** while embracing the rich liturgical heritage of the West.

Unlike the modern drift I observed in other traditions, **Orthodoxy remains steadfast**, committed to the truths handed down from Christ and His Apostles. The

sacraments, prayer, and fasting are no longer just rituals—they are the means by which we participate in the **divine life of God** and are transformed into His likeness.

Glossary of Orthodox Terminology

Apostolic Succession
The unbroken line of spiritual authority passed down from the Apostles through bishops, ensuring the Church remains faithful to the teachings of Christ.

Ancestral Sin
The Orthodox understanding of humanity's inherited fallen nature from Adam and Eve, distinct from the Roman Catholic concept of original sin, emphasizing inherited mortality and corruption rather than guilt.

Baptism
The sacrament of initiation into the Christian life, symbolizing death to sin, spiritual rebirth, and union with Christ. Baptism cleanses the soul and imparts divine grace.

Chrismation
The sacrament that follows baptism, where the newly baptized are anointed with holy oil (chrism) to receive the gift of the Holy Spirit, empowering them for the Christian life. It differs from Roman Catholic Confirmation by being given immediately after baptism.

Divine Liturgy
The central act of Orthodox worship, culminating in the celebration of the Eucharist. It mirrors the heavenly liturgy and unites believers with Christ through the sacraments.

Dormition of the Theotokos

The Orthodox belief that the Virgin Mary, the Theotokos, experienced a natural death and was taken body and soul into heaven by her Son. It contrasts with the Roman Catholic doctrine of the Assumption.

Eucharist

The sacrament of the Body and Blood of Christ, offered during the Divine Liturgy. Orthodox Christians believe in the real presence of Christ, though the concept of transubstantiation is not emphasized, focusing instead on the mystery of union with God.

Fasting

A spiritual discipline practiced by Orthodox Christians to purify the body and soul, preparing believers to receive the sacraments. Fasting is especially significant before receiving the Eucharist.

Filioque

A clause meaning "and the Son," added to the Nicene Creed by the Western Church, leading to theological disputes with Orthodoxy. The Orthodox Church rejects this addition, citing the Council of Ephesus' prohibition of changes to the creed.

Hesychasm

A mystical tradition of prayer and stillness in Orthodox Christianity, focusing on the practice of the Jesus Prayer: "Lord Jesus Christ, Son of God, have mercy on me, a sinner."

Icons

Sacred images used in Orthodox worship as windows to the divine. Icons reflect divine realities, aiding believers in prayer and serving as reminders of the saints' presence and intercession.

Mariology

The theological study of the Virgin Mary, the Theotokos. Orthodox Mariology emphasizes her role in salvation history, her intercessory prayers, and her life as a model for theosis. Orthodox Christianity honors her without developing additional doctrines like the Immaculate Conception.

Original Sin

A doctrine in Roman Catholicism stating that humanity inherits both the guilt and corruption of Adam's sin. In contrast, Orthodoxy teaches ancestral sin, where humans inherit a fallen nature but not personal guilt.

Papal Primacy

The Roman Catholic doctrine that the Pope has supreme authority over the universal Church. Orthodox Christianity rejects this understanding, affirming instead the conciliar model of Church governance, where all bishops hold equal apostolic authority.

Sacraments

Also known as mysteries, sacraments are channels of divine grace that transform believers and bring them closer to God. The seven sacraments include Baptism, Chrismation, Eucharist, Confession, Marriage, Holy Orders, and Anointing of the Sick.

Synergism
The Orthodox belief that salvation involves cooperation between divine grace and human free will. God offers grace, but humans must actively respond through repentance, faith, and good works.

Theosis
The process of becoming one with God through participation in His divine life. Theosis is the ultimate goal of the Christian life, achieved through the sacraments, prayer, fasting, and living a life of virtue.

Theotokos
A title for the Virgin Mary meaning "God-bearer" or "Mother of God." It affirms the Incarnation, emphasizing that Mary gave birth to the God-Man, Jesus Christ.

Transubstantiation
A term used in Roman Catholic theology to describe the change of bread and wine into the Body and Blood of Christ. Orthodox Christianity affirms the real presence in the Eucharist but does not use this term, focusing instead on the mystery of the sacrament.

Western Orthodoxy
A branch of the Orthodox Church that expresses the ancient faith through Western liturgical traditions, such as

the Gregorian and Sarum rites, while remaining faithful to the theological teachings of the undivided Church.

Bibliography

Primary Sources:

- **The Holy Bible (Orthodox Study Bible)**
  New King James Version with Commentary by the Orthodox Church. St. Athanasius Academy of Orthodox Theology, Thomas Nelson, 2008.

- **Philokalia**: The Complete Text
  Compiled by St. Nikodemos of the Holy Mountain and St. Makarios of Corinth. Translated by G. E. H. Palmer, Philip Sherrard, and Kallistos Ware. Faber and Faber, 1979.

- **The Way of a Pilgrim and The Pilgrim Continues His Way**
  Translated by R. M. French. HarperOne, 1992.

- **The Ladder of Divine Ascent**
  By St. John Climacus. Translated by Colm Luibheid and Norman Russell. Paulist Press, 1982.

- **On the Incarnation**
  By St. Athanasius the Great. Translated by John Behr. St. Vladimir's Seminary Press, 2011.

- **The Orthodox Way**

  By Metropolitan Kallistos (Ware). St. Vladimir's
  Seminary Press, 1995.

- **On the Holy Spirit**

  By St. Basil the Great. Translated by David
  Anderson. St. Vladimir's Seminary Press, 1980.

- **The Life of St. Mary of Egypt**

  Written by St. Sophronius, Patriarch of Jerusalem.
  Translated by Benedicta Ward. Cistercian
  Publications, 1991.

- **The Festal Menaion**

  Translated by Mother Mary and Kallistos Ware. St.
  Tikhon's Seminary Press, 1990.

- **The Liturgy of St. John Chrysostom**

  Standard Orthodox Liturgical Text. Holy Cross
  Orthodox Press, 1985.

Secondary Sources:

- **The Orthodox Church: An Introduction to
  Eastern Christianity**

  By Timothy Ware (Metropolitan Kallistos). Penguin
  Books, 1993.

- **For the Life of the World: Sacraments and
  Orthodoxy**

By Alexander Schmemann. St. Vladimir's
Seminary Press, 1997.

- **Becoming Orthodox: A Journey to the Ancient
  Christian Faith**
  By Peter E. Gillquist. Conciliar Press, 1992.

- **The Mystical Theology of the Eastern Church**
  By Vladimir Lossky. St. Vladimir's Seminary
  Press, 1976.

- **The Theology of St. Gregory Palamas**
  By John Meyendorff. St. Vladimir's Seminary
  Press, 1998.

- **The Meaning of Icons**
  By Leonid Ouspensky and Vladimir Lossky. St.
  Vladimir's Seminary Press, 1999.

- **Christ in Eastern Christian Thought**
  By John Meyendorff. St. Vladimir's Seminary
  Press, 1987.

- **The Eucharist: Sacrament of the Kingdom**
  By Alexander Schmemann. St. Vladimir's
  Seminary Press, 2003.

- **Early Christian Doctrines**
  By J. N. D. Kelly. HarperOne, 1978.

- **Orthodox Dogmatic Theology**

  By Fr. Michael Pomazansky. St. Herman of Alaska Brotherhood, 2005.

Patristic Writings and Commentaries:

- **Against Heresies**

  By St. Irenaeus of Lyons. Translated by Dominic J. Unger. Paulist Press, 1992.

- **The City of God**

  By St. Augustine of Hippo. Translated by Henry Bettenson. Penguin Books, 2003.

- **The Sayings of the Desert Fathers**

  Translated by Benedicta Ward. Cistercian Publications, 1984.

- **On the Divine Liturgy**

  By St. Nicholas Cabasilas. Translated by J. M. Hussey and P. A. McNulty. St. Vladimir's Seminary Press, 1997.

- **On the Unity of Christ**

  By St. Cyril of Alexandria. Translated by John McGuckin. St. Vladimir's Seminary Press, 1995.

- **The Four Books of St. John of Damascus**

  Translated by Frederic H. Chase. Catholic University of America Press, 1958.

- **Catechetical Lectures**

  By St. Cyril of Jerusalem. Translated by Edward
  Yarnold. St. Vladimir's Seminary Press, 1980.

Additional Theological Resources:

- **The Doctrine of Deification in the Greek
  Patristic Tradition**

  By Norman Russell. Oxford University Press, 2004.

- **The Eucharist and the Trinity**

  By John D. Zizioulas. St. Vladimir's Seminary
  Press, 1997.

- **The Spirit of Early Christian Thought**

  By Robert Louis Wilken. Yale University Press,
  2005.

- **Living the Liturgy: Reflections on the Eucharist**

  By St. Symeon of Thessalonica. Translated by
  Thomas Carroll. Cistercian Publications, 2006.

- **Orthodox Christian Teaching on Grace and Free
  Will**

  By Dumitru Staniloae. Translated by Ionut Chirila.
  St. Vladimir's Seminary Press, 2002.

- **The Ancestral Sin**

  By John S. Romanides. Ridgewood, 2002.

- **Orthodox Prayer Life: The Interior Way**

  By Matthew the Poor. St. Vladimir's Seminary Press, 2003.

- **The Communion of Love**

  By Matthew the Poor. St. Vladimir's Seminary Press, 1984.

This bibliography provides foundational works used for the creation of the study guide, drawing from a range of scriptural, patristic, and theological texts relevant to Orthodox Christianity, the sacraments, theosis, grace, and the overall spiritual life.

Made in the USA
Monee, IL
06 December 2024

72276210R00177